The
Argentine Temporada Motor Races
1950 to 1960

- in 220 contemporary photos

Hernan Lopez Laiseca

Also from Veloce:

Essential Buyer's Guide Series
Alfa Romeo Giulia GT Coupé (Booker)
Alfa Romeo Giulia Spider (Booker)
Audi TT (Davies)
Austin Seven (Barker)
Big Healeys (Trummel)
BMW E21 3 Series (1975-1983) (Reverente)
BMW E30 3 Series 1981 to 1994 (Hosier)
BMW GS (Henshaw)
BMW X5 (Saunders)
BSA 350 & 500 Unit Construction Singles (Henshaw)
BSA 500 & 650 Twins (Henshaw)
BSA Bantam (Henshaw)
Citroën 2CV (Paxton)
Citroën ID & DS (Heilig)
Cobra Replicas (Ayre)
Corvette C2 Sting Ray 1963-1967 (Falconer)
Ducati Bevel Twins (Falloon)
Ducati Desmodue Twins (Falloon)
Ducati Desmoquattro Twins – 851, 888, 916, 996, 998, ST4 1988 to 2004 (Falloon)
Ducati Overhead Camshaft Singles, "The Book of the (Falloon)
Fiat 500 & 600 (Bobbitt)
Ford Capri (Paxton)
Ford Escort Mk1 & Mk2 (Williamson)
Ford Mustang – First Generation 1964 to 1973 (Cook)
Ford Mustang – Fifth generation/S197 (Cook)
Ford RS Cosworth Sierra & Escort (Williamson)
Harley-Davidson Big Twins (Henshaw)
Hinckley Triumph triples & fours 750, 900, 955, 1000, 1050, 1200 – 1991-2009 (Henshaw)
Honda CBR FireBlade (Henshaw)
Honda CBR600 Hurricane (Henshaw)
Honda SOHC Fours 1969-1984 (Henshaw)
Jaguar E-Type 3.8 & 4.2-litre (Crespin)
Jaguar E-type V12 5.3-litre (Crespin)
Jaguar Mark 1 & 2 (All models including Daimler 2.5-litre V8) 1955 to 1969 (Thorley)
Jaguar S-Type – 1999 to 2007 (Thorley)
Jaguar X-Type – 2001 to 2009 (Thorley)
Jaguar XJ-S (Crespin)
Jaguar XJ6, XJ8 & XJR (Thorley)
Jaguar XK 120, 140 & 150 (Thorley)
Jaguar XK8 & XKR (1996-2005) (Thorley)
Jaguar/Daimler XJ 1994-2003 (Crespin)
Jaguar/Daimler XJ40 (Crespin)
Jaguar/Daimler XJ6, XJ12 & Sovereign (Crespin)
Kawasaki Z1 & Z900 (Orritt)
Land Rover Series I, II & IIA (Thurman)
Land Rover Series III (Thurman)
Lotus Seven replicas & Caterham 7: 1973-2013 (Hawkins)
Mazda MX-5 Miata (Mk1 1989-97 & Mk2 98-2001) (Crook)
Mercedes Benz Pagoda 230SL, 250SL & 280SL roadsters & coupés (Bass)
Mercedes-Benz 280-560SL & SLC (Bass)
MG Midget & A-H Sprite (Horler)
MG TD, TF & TF1500 (Jones)
MGA 1955-1962 (Crosier)
MGB & MGB GT (Williams)
MGF & MG TF (Hawkins)
Mini (Paxton)
Morris Minor & 1000 (Newell)
Moto Guzzi 2-valve big twins (Falloon)
New Mini (Collins)
Norton Commando (Henshaw)
Peugeot 205 GTI (Blackburn)
Porsche 911 (964) (Streather)
Porsche 911 (993) (Streather)
Porsche 911 (996) (Streather)
Porsche 911 Carrera 3.2 (Streather)
Porsche 911SC (Streather)
Porsche 924 – All models 1976 to 1988 (Hodgkins)
Porsche 928 (Hemmings)
Porsche 930 Turbo & 911 (930) Turbo (Streather)
Porsche 944 (Higgins)
Porsche 986 Boxster (Streather)
Porsche 987 Boxster & Cayman (Streather)
Rolls-Royce Silver Shadow & Bentley T-Series (Bobbitt)
Subaru Impreza (Hobbs)
Triumph 350 & 500 Twins (Henshaw)
Triumph Bonneville (Henshaw)
Triumph Herald & Vitesse (Davies)
Triumph Spitfire & GT6 (Baugues)
Triumph Stag (Mort)
Triumph Thunderbird, Trophy & Tiger (Henshaw)
Triumph TR6 (Williams)
Triumph TR7 & TR8 (Williams)
Vespa Scooters – Classic 2-stroke models 1960-2008 (Paxton)
Volvo 700/900 Series (Beavis)
VW Beetle (Cservenka & Copping)
VW Bus (Cservenka & Copping)
VW Golf GTI (Cservenka & Copping)

Those Were The Days ... Series
Alpine Trials & Rallies 1910-1973 (Pfundner)
American 'Independent' Automakers – AMC to Willys 1945 to 1960 (Mort)
American Station Wagons – The Golden Era 1950-1975 (Mort)
American Trucks of the 1950s (Mort)
American Trucks of the 1960s (Mort)
American Woodies 1928-1953 (Mort)
Anglo-American Cars from the 1930s to the 1970s (Mort)
Austerity Motoring (Bobbitt)
Austins, The last real (Peck)
Brighton National Speed Trials (Gardiner)
British and European Trucks of the 1970s (Peck)
British Drag Racing – The early years (Pettitt)
British Lorries of the 1950s (Bobbitt)
British Lorries of the 1960s (Bobbitt)
British Touring Car Racing (Collins)
British Police Cars (Walker)
British Woodies (Peck)
Café Racer Phenomenon, The (Walker)
Don Hayter's MGB Story – The birth of the MGB in MG's Abingdon Design & Development Office (Hayter)
Drag Bike Racing in Britain – From the mid '60s to the mid '80s (Lee)
Dune Buggy Phenomenon, The (Hale)
Dune Buggy Phenomenon Volume 2, The (Hale)
Endurance Racing at Silverstone in the 1970s & 1980s (Parker)
Hot Rod & Stock Car Racing in Britain in the 1980s (Neil)
Last Real Austins 1946-1959, The (Peck)
Mercedes-Benz Trucks (Peck)
MG's Abingdon Factory (Moylan)
Motor Racing at Brands Hatch in the Seventies (Parker)
Motor Racing at Brands Hatch in the Eighties (Parker)
Motor Racing at Crystal Palace (Collins)
Motor Racing at Goodwood in the Sixties (Gardiner)
Motor Racing at Nassau in the 1950s & 1960s (O'Neil)
Motor Racing at Oulton Park in the 1960s (McFadyen)
Motor Racing at Oulton Park in the 1970s (McFadyen)
Motor Racing at Thruxton in the 1970s (Grant-Braham)
Motor Racing at Thruxton in the 1980s (Grant-Braham)
Superprix – The Story of Birmingham Motor Race (Page & Collins)
Three Wheelers (Bobbitt)

Rally Giants Series
Audi Quattro (Robson)
Austin Healey 100-6 & 3000 (Robson)
Fiat 131 Abarth (Robson)
Ford Escort MkI (Robson)
Ford Escort RS Cosworth & World Rally Car (Robson)
Ford Escort RS1800 (Robson)
Lancia Delta 4WD/Integrale (Robson)
Lancia Stratos (Robson)
Mini Cooper/Mini Cooper S (Robson)
Peugeot 205 T16 (Robson)
Saab 96 & V4 (Robson)
Subaru Impreza (Robson)
Toyota Celica GT4 (Robson)

Biographies
A Chequered Life – Graham Warner and the Chequered Flag (Hesletine)
Amédée Gordini ... a true racing legend (Smith)
André Lefebvre, and the cars he created at Voisin and Citroën (Beck)
Chris Carter at Large – Stories from a lifetime in motorcycle racing (Carter & Skelton)
Cliff Allison, The Official Biography of – From the Fells to Ferrari (Gauld)
Edward Turner – The Man Behind the Motorcycles (Clew)
Driven by Desire – The Desiré Wilson Story
First Principles – The Official Biography of Keith Duckworth (Burr)
Inspired to Design – F1 cars, Indycars & racing tyres: the autobiography of Nigel Bennett (Bennett)
Jack Sears, The Official Biography of – Gentleman Jack (Gauld)
Jim Redman – 6 Times World Motorcycle Champion: The Autobiography (Redman)
John Chatham – 'Mr Big Healey' – The Official Biography (Burr)
The Lee Noble Story (Wilkins)
Mason's Motoring Mayhem – Tony Mason's hectic life in motorsport and television (Mason)
Raymond Mays' Magnificent Obsession (Apps)
Pat Moss Carlsson Story, The – Harnessing Horsepower (Turner)
Tony Robinson – The biography of a race mechanic (Wagstaff)
Virgil Exner – Visioneer: The Official Biography of Virgil M Exner Designer Extraordinaire (Grist)

General
1½-litre GP Racing 1961-1965 (Whitelock)
AC Two-litre Saloons & Buckland Sportscars (Archibald)
Alfa Romeo 155/156/147 Competition Touring Cars (Collins)
Alfa Romeo Giulia Coupé GT & GTA (Tipler)
Alfa Romeo Montreal – The dream car that came true (Taylor)
Alfa Romeo Montreal – The Essential Companion (Classic Reprint of 500 copies) (Taylor)
Alfa Tipo 33 (McDonough & Collins)
Alpine & Renault – The Development of the Revolutionary Turbo F1 Car 1968 to 1979 (Smith)
Alpine & Renault – The Sports Prototypes 1963 to 1969 (Smith)
Alpine & Renault – The Sports Prototypes 1973 to 1978 (Smith)
Anatomy of the Works Minis (Moylan)
Armstrong-Siddeley (Smith)
Art Deco and British Car Design (Down)
Autodrome (Collins & Ireland)
Autodrome 2 (Collins & Ireland)
Automotive A-Z, Lane's Dictionary of Automotive Terms (Lane)
Automotive Mascots (Kay & Springate)
Bahamas Speed Weeks, The (O'Neil)
Bentley Continental, Corniche and Azure (Bennett)
Bentley MkVI, Rolls-Royce Silver Wraith, Dawn & Cloud/ Bentley R & S-Series (Nutland)
Bluebird CN7 (Stevens)
BMC Competitions Department Secrets (Turner, Chambers & Browning)
BMW 5-Series (Cranswick)
BMW Z-Cars (Taylor)
BMW Boxer Twins 1970-1995 Bible, The (Falloon)
BMW Cafe Racers (Cloesen)
BMW Custom Motorcycles – Choppers, Cruisers, Bobbers, Trikes & Quads (Cloesen)
BMW – The Power of M (Vivian)
Bonjour – Is this Italy? (Turner)
British 250cc Racing Motorcycles (Pereira)
British at Indianapolis, The (Wagstaff)
British Cars, The Complete Catalogue of, 1895-1975 (Culshaw & Horrobin)
British Custom Motorcycles – The Brit Chop – choppers, cruisers, bobbers & trikes (Cloesen)
BRM – A Mechanic's Tale (Salmon)
BRM V16 (Ludvigsen)
BSA Bantam Bible, The (Henshaw)
BSA Motorcycles – the final evolution (Jones)
Bugatti Type 40 (Price)
Bugatti 46/50 Updated Edition (Price & Arbey)
Bugatti T44 & T49 (Price & Arbey)
Bugatti 57 2nd Edition (Price)
Bugatti Type 57 Grand Prix – A Celebration (Tomlinson)
Caravan, Improve & Modify Your (Porter)
Caravans, The Illustrated History 1919-1959 (Jenkinson)
Caravans, The Illustrated History From 1960 (Jenkinson)
Carrera Panamericana, La (Tipler)
Chrysler 300 – America's Most Powerful Car 2nd Edition (Ackerson)
Chrysler PT Cruiser (Ackerson)
Citroën DS (Bobbitt)
Classic British Car Electrical Systems (Astley)
Cobra – The Real Thing! (Legate)
Competition Car Aerodynamics 3rd Edition (McBeath)
Concept Cars, How to illustrate and design (Dewey)
Cortina – Ford's Bestseller (Robson)
Coventry Climax Racing Engines (Hammill)
Daily Mirror 1970 World Cup Rally 40, The (Robson)
Daimler SP250 New Edition (Long)
Datsun Fairlady Roadster to 280ZX – The Z-Car Story (Long)
Dino – The V6 Ferrari (Long)
Dodge Challenger & Plymouth Barracuda (Grist)
Dodge Charger – Enduring Thunder (Ackerson)
Dodge Dynamite! (Grist)
Dorset from the Sea – The Jurassic Coast from Lyme Regis to Old Harry Rocks photographed from its best viewpoint (Belasco)
Dorset from the Sea – The Jurassic Coast from Lyme Regis to Old Harry Rocks photographed from its best viewpoint (souvenir edition) (Belasco)
Draw & Paint Cars – How to (Gardiner)
Drive on the Wild Side, A – 20 Extreme Driving Adventures From Around the World (Weaver)
Ducati 750 Bible, The (Falloon)
Ducati 750 SS 'round-case' 1974, The Book of the (Falloon)
Ducati 860, 900 and Mille Bible, The (Falloon)
Ducati Monster Bible (New Updated & Revised Edition), The (Falloon)
Dune Buggy, Building A – The Essential Manual (Shakespeare)
Dune Buggy Files (Hale)
Dune Buggy Handbook (Hale)
East German Motor Vehicles in Pictures (Suhr/Weinreich)
Fast Ladies – Female Racing Drivers 1888 to 1970 (Bouzanquet)
Fate of the Sleeping Beauties, The (op de Weegh/Hottendorff/ op de Weegh)
Ferrari 288 GTO, The Book of the (Sackey)
Ferrari 333 SP (O'Neil)
Fiat & Abarth 124 Spider & Coupé (Tipler)
Fiat & Abarth 500 & 600 – 2nd Edition (Bobbitt)
Fiats, Great Small (Ward)
Fine Art of the Motorcycle Engine, The (Peirce)
Ford Cleveland 335-Series V8 engine 1970 to 1982 – The Essential Source Book (Hammill)
Ford F100/F150 Pick-up 1948-1996 (Ackerson)
Ford F150 Pick-up 1997-2005 (Ackerson)
Ford GT – Then, and Now (Streather)
Ford GT40 (Legate)
Ford Model Y (Roberts)
Ford Small Block V8 Racing Engines 1962-1970 – The Essential Source Book (Hammill)
Ford Thunderbird From 1954, The Book of the (Long)
Formula 5000 Motor Racing, Back then ... and back now (Lawson)
Forza Minardi! (Vigar)
France: the essential guide for car enthusiasts – 200 things for the car enthusiast to see and do (Parish)
From Crystal Palace to Red Square – A Hapless Biker's Road to Russia (Turner)
Funky Mopeds (Skelton)
Grand Prix Ferrari – The Years of Enzo Ferrari's Power, 1948-1980 (Pritchard)
Grand Prix Ford – DFV-powered Formula 1 Cars (Pritchard)
GT – The World's Best GT Cars 1953-73 (Dawson)
Hillclimbing & Sprinting – The Essential Manual (Short & Wilkinson)
Honda NSX (Long)
Inside the Rolls-Royce & Bentley Styling Department – 1971 to 2001 (Hull)
Intermeccanica – The Story of the Prancing Bull (McCredie & Reisner)
Italian Cafe Racers (Cloesen)
Italian Custom Motorcycles (Cloesen)
Jaguar, The Rise of (Price)
Jaguar XJ 220 – The Inside Story (Moreton)
Jaguar XJ-S, The Book of the (Long)
Jeep CJ (Ackerson)
Jeep Wrangler (Ackerson)
Karmann-Ghia Coupé & Convertible (Bobbitt)
Kawasaki Triples Bible, The (Walker)
Kawasaki Z1 Story, The (Sheehan)
Kris Meeke – Intercontinental Rally Challenge Champion (McBride)
Lamborghini Miura Bible, The (Sackey)
Lamborghini Urraco, The Book of the (Landsem)
Lambretta Bible, The (Davies)
Lancia 037 (Collins)
Lancia Delta HF Integrale (Blaettel & Wagner)
Land Rover Series III Reborn (Porter)
Land Rover, The Half-ton Military (Cook)
Laverda Twins & Triples Bible 1968-1986 (Falloon)
Lea-Francis Story, The (Price)
Le Mans Panoramic (Ireland)
Lexus Story, The (Long)
Little book of microcars, the (Quellin)
Little book of smart, the – New Edition (Jackson)
Little book of trikes, the (Quellin)
Lola – The Illustrated History (1957-1977) (Starkey)
Lola – All the Sports Racing & Single-seater Racing Cars 1978-1997 (Starkey)
Lola T70 – The Racing History & Individual Chassis Record – 4th Edition (Starkey)
Lotus 49 (Oliver)
Marketingmobiles, The Wonderful Wacky World of (Hale)
Maserati 250F In Focus (Pritchard)
Mazda MX-5/Miata 1.6 Enthusiast's Workshop Manual (Grainger & Shoemark)
Mazda MX-5/Miata 1.8 Enthusiast's Workshop Manual (Grainger & Shoemark)
The book of the Mazda MX-5 Miata – The 'Mk1' NA-series 1988 to 1997 (Long)
Mazda MX-5 Miata Roadster (Long)
Maximum Mini (Booij)
Meet the English (Bowie)
Mercedes-Benz SL – R230 series 2001 to 2011 (Long)
Mercedes-Benz SL – W113-series 1963-1971 (Long)
Mercedes-Benz SL & SLC – 107-series 1971-1989 (Long)
Mercedes-Benz SLK – R170 series 1996-2004 (Long)
Mercedes-Benz SLK – R171 series 2004-2011 (Long)
Mercedes-Benz W123-series – All models 1976 to 1986 (Long)
MGA (Price Williams)
MGB & MGB GT– Expert Guide (Auto-doc Series) (Williams)
MGB Electrical Systems Updated & Revised Edition (Astley)
Micro Caravans (Jenkinson)
Micro Trucks (Mort)
Microcars at Large! (Quellin)
Mini Cooper – The Real Thing! (Tipler)
Mini Minor to Asia Minor (West)
Mitsubishi Lancer Evo, The Road Car & WRC Story (Long)
Montlhéry, The Story of the Paris Autodrome (Boddy)
Morgan Maverick (Lawrence)
Morgan 3 Wheeler – back to the future!, The (Dron)
Morris Minor, 60 Years on the Road (Newell)
Moto Guzzi Sport & Le Mans Bible, The (Falloon)
Motor Movies – The Posters! (Veysey)
Motor Racing – Reflections of a Lost Era (Carter)
Motor Racing – The Pursuit of Victory 1930-1962 (Carter)
Motor Racing – The Pursuit of Victory 1963-1972 (Wyatt/ Sears)
Motor Racing Heroes – The Stories of 100 Greats (Newman)
Motorcycle Apprentice (Cakebread)
Motorcycle GP Racing in the 1960s (Pereira)
Motorcycle Road & Racing Chassis Designs (Noakes)
Motorhomes, The Illustrated History (Jenkinson)
Motorsport In colour, 1950s (Wainwright)
MV Agusta Fours, The book of the classic (Falloon)
N.A.R.T. – A concise history of the North American Racing Team 1957 to 1983 (O'Neil)
Nissan 300ZX & 350Z – The Z-Car Story (Long)
Nissan GT-R Supercar: Born to race (Gorodji)
Northeast American Sports Car Races 1950-1959 (O'Neil)
Nothing Runs – Misadventures in the Classic, Collectable & Exotic Car Biz (Slutsky)
Off-Road Giants! (Volume 1) – Heroes of 1960s Motorcycle Sport (Westlake)
Off-Road Giants! (Volume 2) – Heroes of 1960s Motorcycle Sport (Westlake)
Off-Road Giants! (volume 3) – Heroes of 1960s Motorcycle Sport (Westlake)
Pass the Theory and Practical Driving Tests (Gibson & Hoole)
Peking to Paris 2007 (Young)
Pontiac Firebird (Cranswick)
Porsche Boxster (Long)
Porsche 356 (2nd Edition) (Long)
Porsche 908 (Födisch, Neßhöver, Roßbach, Schwarz & Roßbach)
Porsche 911 Carrera – The Last of the Evolution (Corlett)
Porsche 911R, RS & RSR, 4th Edition (Starkey)
Porsche 911, The Book of the (Long)
Porsche 911SC 'Super Carrera' – The Essential Companion (Streather)
Porsche 914 & 914-6: The Definitive History of the Road & Competition Cars (Long)
Porsche 924 (Long)
The Porsche 924 Carreras – evolution to excellence (Smith)
Porsche 928 (Long)
Porsche 944 (Long)
Porsche 964, 993 & 996 Data Plate Code Breaker (Streather)
Porsche 993 'King Of Porsche' – The Essential Companion (Streather)
Porsche 996 'Supreme Porsche' – The Essential Companion (Streather)
Porsche Racing Cars – 1953 to 1975 (Long)
Porsche Racing Cars – 1976 to 2005 (Long)
Porsche – The Rally Story (Meredith)
Porsche: Three Generations of Genius (Meredith)
Preston Tucker & Others (Linde)
RAC Rally Action! (Gardiner)
RACING COLOURS – MOTOR RACING COMPOSITIONS 1908-2009 (Newman)
Racing Line – British motorcycle racing in the golden age of the big single (Guntrip)
Rallye Sport Fords: The Inside Story (Moreton)
Renewable Energy Home Handbook, The (Porter)
Roads with a View – England's greatest views and how to find them by road (Corfield)
Rolls-Royce Silver Shadow/Bentley T Series Corniche & Camargue – Revised & Enlarged Edition (Bobbitt)
Rolls-Royce Silver Spirit, Silver Spur & Bentley Mulsanne 2nd Edition (Bobbitt)
Runways & Racers (O'Neil)
Russian Motor Vehicles – Soviet Limousines 1930-2003 (Kelly)
Russian Motor Vehicles – The Czarist Period 1784 to 1917 (Kelly)
RX-7 – Mazda's Rotary Engine Sportscar (Updated & Revised New Edition) (Long)
Scooters & Microcars, The A-Z of Popular (Dan)
Scooter Lifestyle (Grainger)
SCOOTER MANIA! – Recollections of the Isle of Man International Scooter Rally (Jackson)
Singer Story: Cars, Commercial Vehicles, Bicycles & Motorcycle (Atkinson)
Sleeping Beauties USA – abandoned classic cars & trucks (Marek)
SM – Citroën's Maserati-engined Supercar (Long & Claverol)
Speedway – Auto racing's ghost tracks (Collins & Ireland)
Sprite Caravans, The Story of (Jenkinson)
Standard Motor Company, The Book of the
Subaru Impreza: The Road Car And WRC Story (Long)
Supercar, How to Build your own (Thompson)
Tales from the Toolbox (Oliver)
Tatra – The Legacy of Hans Ledwinka, Updated & Enlarged Collector's Edition of 1500 copies (Margolius & Henry)
Taxi! The Story of the 'London' Taxicab (Bobbitt)
Toleman Story, The (Hilton)
Toyota Celica & Supra, The Book of Toyota's Sports Coupés (Long)
Toyota MR2 Coupés & Spyders (Long)
Triumph Bonneville Bible (59-83) (Henshaw)
Triumph Bonneville!, Save the – The inside story of the Meriden Workers' Co-op (Rosamond)
Triumph Motorcycles & the Meriden Factory (Hancox)
Triumph Speed Twin & Thunderbird Bible (Woolridge)
Triumph Tiger Cub Bible (Estall)
Triumph Trophy Bible (Woolridge)
Triumph TR6 (Kimberley)
TT Talking – The TT's most exciting era – As seen by Manx Radio TT's lead commentator 2004-2012 (Lambert)
Two Summers – The Mercedes-Benz W196R Racing Car (Ackerson)
TWR Story, The – Group A (Hughes & Scott)
Unraced (Collins)
Velocette Motorcycles – MSS to Thruxton – New Third Edition (Burris)
Vespa – The Story of a Cult Classic in Pictures (Uhlig)
Volkswagen Bus Book, The (Bobbitt)
Volkswagen Bus or Van to Camper, How to Convert (Porter)
Volkswagens of the World (Glen)
VW Beetle Cabriolet – The full story of the convertible Beetle (Bobbitt)
VW Beetle – The Car of the 20th Century (Copping)
VW Bus – 40 Years of Splitties, Bays & Wedges (Copping)
VW Bus Book, The (Bobbitt)
VW Golf: Five Generations of Fun (Copping & Cservenka)
VW – The Air-cooled Era (Copping)
VW T5 Camper Conversion Manual (Porter)
VW Campers (Copping)
You & Your Jaguar XK8/XKR – Buying, Enjoying, Maintaining, Modifying – New Edition (Thorley)
Which Oil? – Choosing the right oils & greases for your antique, vintage, veteran, classic or collector car (Michell)
Works Minis, The Last (Purves & Brenchley)
Works Rally Mechanic (Moylan)

Veloce's other imprints:

BATTLE CRY!

Hubble & Hattie

For post publication news, updates and amendments relating to this book please visit www.veloce.co.uk/books/V4828

www.veloce.co.uk

First published in December 2015 by Veloce Publishing Limited, Veloce House, Parkway Farm Business Park, Middle Farm Way, Poundbury, Dorchester DT1 3AR, England. Fax 01305 268864 / e-mail info@veloce.co.uk / web www.veloce.co.uk or www.velocebooks.com. ISBN: 978-1-845848-28-6 UPC: 6-36847-04828-0.
 British Library Cataloguing in Publication Data – A catalogue record for this book is available from the British Library. Typesetting, design and page make-up all by Veloce Publishing Ltd on Apple Mac.
Printed in India by Replika Press

The
Argentine Temporada Motor Races

1950 to 1960

– in 220 contemporary photos

VELOCE PUBLISHING
THE PUBLISHER OF FINE AUTOMOTIVE BOOKS

Contents

Acknowledgements: Unless otherwise stated, the images in this book are the property of the author or are used with permission from Pique Lopez, Automovil Club Argentino, Timoteo Lopez Laiseca, and Marcos Lopez Laiseca. Publisher's note: the contemporary images appearing in this book were drawn from many sources and, as presented, varied enormously in quality and state of preservation. Where possible we have enhanced the images, but have tried to leave some of the patina which evidences how these images have been saved and treasured by their owners for many years.

Prologue

Between 1935 and 1941 Argentine motor racing had its golden age, with more than 30 races per year on loose surface tracks called 'park type' circuits, scattered around the interior of the country. There were so many requests to organise such races that there was insufficient time to prepare a calendar of events without clashing dates.

It was during this period that the first competitions, with invited international drivers, actually began. In 1935, for instance, in the '500 Miles of Rafaela' event, the Brazilian drivers Baron Manuel de Teffé, Francisco Chico Landi and Cicero Marquez Porto were all invited.

In 1936, the City of Buenos Aires Grand Prix, won by Carlos Arzani (Alfa Romeo), was run on a circuit of part asphalt, and part soil, which had been especially designed for this race in the Costanera suburb of Buenos Aires, with the presence of Brazilian drivers Manuel de Teffé and Domingo Lopes.

In 1941 the second Grand Prix of Buenos Aires took place, but this time it was run on the Retiro circuit in the city centre, on completely paved surfaces. Brazilian drivers also took part, and the winner was José Canzani in an Alfa Romeo.

These international races proved that with adequate organisation and control, streets and avenues in Argentinian cities could be used for car racing: racing which would challenge drivers and their European-built machines. However, when World War Two exploded in Europe this glorious era was brought to an end.

1947 – I Gran Premio Ciudad de Buenos Aires

The Alfa Romeo 308 of Varzi arrived by plane from Brazil. Racing in Argentina meant good prize money, and the opportunity to sell cars and engines to local drivers.

The Italian journalists Filippini and Borgonova (in the white suit) were the main promoters of the Temporadas. They are seen here with Italian drivers Varzi and Villoresi.

In Europe, motor racing returned in 1946. In Argentina, however, returning after five years was not going to be easy. Pancho Borgonovo was placed at the head of the Automobile Club Argentino (ACA) Racing Commission to handle the restart of activity. He began by making contacts in Europe to see if several races could be organised. Before long, teams from Europe became interested, and some decided to cross the Atlantic with their cars.

But why were these races organised? Because in Argentina, at that time, motor racing was a growing passion, rather like football. One of the local objectives of these races was to watch, learn, get experience and gain knowledge. There were also several ingenious and capable local mechanics and drivers who wanted to measure themselves against the drivers and machines of the European elite.

'Park type' circuits were still used for these races, basically because they were available, and because local cars had been engineered for the combination of surfaces. These, though, were not familiar to European and United States teams.

Argentinian promoters could not immediately escape from the traditional circuits as, initially, neither financial resources nor technology were available to create dedicated race circuits. However, what Argentina already had was a large number of public parks with asphalted paths or pavements that could conveniently be used for these races.

The first international season began on 9 February 1947, with drivers and European cars taking part in two races for cars called 'Special' or 'Grand Prix' – one on the Retiro circuit and the other one in the Parque Independencia in Rosario city. Among the visitors were two personalities who captured most attention: Achille Varzi and Luigi ('Gigi') Villoresi, the first driving a 3000cc Alfa Romeo, the second with a modern Maserati 4CL.

The race is remembered because of the battle for the lead between Villoresi and Varzi. It was resolved on the very last

Continues on page 12

The Maserati 4CL of Villoresi in the pits, while George Raph awaits his 6CM.

Hand painting competition – adding numbers to the Alfa Romeo.

Villoresi in the lead with the Maserati 4CL, followed by Pessatti with the Alfa Romeo 8C-35 and Landi with his Alfa Romeo 308.

1947 – I Copa de acción de San Lorenzo

Villoresi and Raph went to Rosario by train for the second race of the season.

1948 – II Gran Premio Gral Juan Domingo Perón

Start of the final. Gálvez (Alfa Romeo 308) takes the lead, followed by Farina (Maserati 8CL), Varzi, Landi and Villoresi (2nd line), Rosa, Ruggeri, Fangio (3rd line), Bizio, Raph (4th line), Platé (5th line).

Varzi in the impressive Alfa Romeo 12C-37.

Wimille with the Alfa Romeo 308 in which Varzi had led the previous year, but with new reconditioned body, and now painted blue.

Villoresi followed by Varzi in the circuit of the Palermo forest.

lap, with a difference of just one second in favour of Villoresi. Behind was Oscar Gálvez (Alfa Romeo) who started out in the lead to the great delight of everyone present, but who had to retire a few laps later. In the second race, in Rosario, the winner was Varzi.

The retired Argentinian Carlos Arzani then chose the Palermo forests and the Mar del Plata circuits to join the international season of 1948. The Palermo was a circuit with roundabouts and many types of closed and open curves. The Mar del Plata was designed as a circuit of about four kilometres in the area of El Torreón, bordering the Atlantic Ocean in two places, with tunnels, ascents and descents, and with the atmosphere of Monte Carlo. No fewer than 200,000 people travelled to see these races. For this season

Gálvez (14) and Farina (16). The first race in Palermo became a major attraction for the public.

Villoresi in the Maserati 4CL of the Scuderia Milano, heading to victory.

1948 – I Gran Premio Internacional San Martin – Mar del Plata

The start at the top of the circuit with Villoresi, Farina and Wimille in the front row.

Shades of Monaco. A panoramic view of the Torreon circuit. More than 2000 people watched the race.

Gálvez (Alfa Romeo 308), Varzi (Alfa Romeo 12C-37) and Wimille (Alfa Romeo 308) next to the sea.

Eitel Cantoni (5) in his Maserati 4CM at the first corner of the circuit, followed by Pedro Llano (6) Maserati 4CM, Farina Maserati 8CL and Villoresi Maserati 4CL.

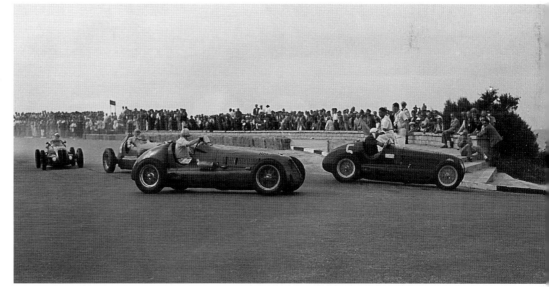

Fangio in a Maserati 4 CL passing Villoresi in another Maserati 4CL on the main straight.

The winner, Farina, with the Maserati 8CL beside the Atlantic Ocean.

Fangio with the Maserati 4 CL.

Farina and Villoresi at speed.

**Gigi Villoresi took pole position, but had
to abandon the race.**

Varzi, Villoresi, 'Raph,' Platé, Farina, Wimille, Landi and
Ruggeri all registered to race, along with Argentinian Gálvez
and Juan Manuel Fangio, who was in his first race in a
special car.

In 1949 the foreign drivers requested a schedule which
would allow them to come to Argentina, to travel for 20 days
in luxurious comfort, and to be a part of the famous Buenos
Aires nightlife. They also had the right to negotiate good
premiums for race starts, and to sell their cars afterwards.

This season European guests were Alberto Ascari, Luigi
Villoresi, Reg Parnell, 'B Bira,' Pascual Puopolo, Giuseppe
Farina and Jean Pierre Wimille. Tragically, Wimille lost his
life during the practice sessions for the first race in Palermo.

Joining them were the Argentinians Bucci, Rosa,
Malusardi, Bizio, Fernandez, Gálvez, Campos, González
and Fangio, among others. Gálvez won at Palermo on 6
February in the rain, while Fangio did the same in Mar del
Plata, winning his first Grand Prix car race.

1948 – II Copa de acción de San Lorenzo – Rosario

The winner, Jean Pierre Wimille, in a Simca Gordini T15.

Gálvez in the lead with the Alfa Romeo 308, followed by Fangio in the Simca Gordini T11.

1949 – III Gran Premio Juan Domingo Perón y de la Republica Argentina – Palermo

The winner, Alberto Ascari, in the Maserati 4CLT.

Benedicto Campos with the Maserati 4CL of the Automovil Club Argentino, followed by Ascari (Scuderia Ambrosiana Maserati 4CLT) in the Palermo forests, full of spectators.

New races were being developed every year to reflect the greater interest from the public and from race drivers. From 1953 the construction in Buenos Aires of the Autódromo 17 de Octubre, allowed the organisers to run events scoring points for the Formula One and Sports cars World Championships, which ended the old days of 'park type' circuits, and was the beginning of a recognised place in the world motorsport calendar.

These international races immediately gave a lot to motorsports. For example, the first victory by a Ferrari outside of Europe was in the 1948 Rosario event, where Farina used a model 125C. The first F1 triumph of a rear-engined car came with the Cooper Climax of Stirling Moss in 1958. These events also hosted the only appearance after the war of the famous 1938-1939 W154 Mercedes-Benz cars, in 1951. They also saw the debut in 1954, of one of the most impressive cars in the history of motor racing: the Maserati 250F. And then there was also the rise of the driver who was already nearing his 40th birthday, but probably did not have any rivals in Europe. That was Juan Manuel Fangio.

This book draws on many stories. Research in archives, libraries and collections allowed collation of a huge amount of detail regarding the events of the time. This work is a sincere tribute to the heroes who allowed us to discover and enjoy the unique world of race cars with their exploits.

Now men, cars and circuits are less glamorous, motor racing is 'colder' and is more technological than in these golden eras, but when the chequered flag drops, the magic, the passion and sport still come through at full speed.

1949 – II Gran Premio Internacional San Martin

The start of the race with Fangio in the Maserati, alone in the lead, heading towards his first victory in a Grand Prix car.

1950

Four wins for Ferrari 125

The 1950 season began with a race on 18 December, 1949, when the presence of all the best European racers and Juan Manuel Fangio demonstrated Argentinian motorsport's seriousness of intent. Ferrari brought three official machines to Argentina, together with a fourth car for the Automóvil Club Argentino Team to run, this being especially painted with the Argentine colours as a gift to Evita Perón. They completed the list of cars: 15 Maseratis, two Alfa Romeos and two Talbots. The new drivers for this season were Clemente Biondetti, Piero Carini, Dorino Serafini, Piero Taruffi, Louis Chiron and Philippe Étancelin.

1949 – IV Gran Premio Juan Domingo Perón

The Italians (second left to right) Villoresi, Farina and Ascari were frequent visitors to the Temporada.

Preparing the cars of the Argentine team in the Argentine Automobile Club.

The fourth Juan Domingo Perón Grand Prix was scheduled over 35 laps on the Palermo circuit, which was 4.865km long. The race began at 4:45pm, and it was Ascari who shone first after sprinting off the line, followed by Villoresi, who led Fangio at the first corner. After the first lap Ascari and Villoresi escaped from Fangio, followed by Campos,

Nino Farina, with the Maserati 4CLT, started in the front row, but retired on lap 16.

González and Farina. Parnell and Whitehead lagged well behind in the last places.

Ascari was moving away at two seconds per lap in the lead. Then on lap 16, Fangio began attacking Villoresi, to overtake him on lap 20 and finally set a new lap record, getting down to a time of 2min 29.6sec, but the fate of the race was cast ...

The race ended with Ascari in first place, and Fangio and Villoresi in second and third respectively. Campos would reach fourth, but was one lap behind. José Froilán

Cantoni pursued by a newcomer in Grand Prix machines, Jose Froilán González, with a Maserati 4CL. The Argentine came fifth despite a penalty for running without head protection.

Top: Seconds before the start. Villoresi (right) sat on pole, alongside Ascari, both with Ferraris. Next left is Farina with a Maserati, and then Fangio with a Ferrari to complete the first row.
Above: At the start Ascari's Ferrari 166 FLis next to the Maserati 4CLT of Farina as the flag drops.

B Bira (Maserati 4CLT), of Scuderia Platé, finished in sixth place.

González was fifth, ahead of Prince Bira who had the first of the modern Maseratis. Even so, the public almost caused a real tragedy, by invading the track when the winner came in to stop at the pits. Bira had to perform several manoeuvres to avoid hitting people and wounded two policemen.

Alberto Ascari (looking exhausted) took a clear victory over Juan Manuel Fangio on the Lakes of Palermo circuit.

1950 – IV Gran Premio Extraordinario Maria Eva Duarte de Perón – Palermo

A medical test for Fangio before the race.

Peter Whitehead and his Ferrari 125C.

After Christmas and New Year, the Maria Eva Duarte de Perón Grand Prix took place in Palermo. Fangio was fastest in the qualifying sessions. In the race itself, Fangio went ahead, followed by Villoresi and Serafini. Ascari made a full spin at the start, but fortunately the rest of the cars did not touch Ascari's car during that uncontrolled spin. A few laps later Ascari had to retire following a radiator breakage.

Left: The Frenchman Louis Rosier, with his Talbot T26C, finished in seventh place.

Below: The Maseratis of Emanuel de Graffenried (30), Bira (42) and Clemente Biondetti (28).

Reg Parnell with the Maserati 4CLT.

Early in the race, Villoresi and Fangio got away from the field. Fangio set the lap record at 2min 28.8sec, but, by lap 10 when he had pulled out an 18 second lead over the Italian, he had to make a pit stop with problems with the left-side rear wheel. The mechanics took two and a half minutes to change the wheel, which left the race gifted to Villoresi.

Juan Manuel Fangio, Ascari, Villoresi and Serafini in the front row, all in Ferraris.

Within a few metres of the start, Ascari could not control the Ferrari: he suffered an uncontrollable spin and collected the bales. He retired a few laps later with a broken radiator.

Pit stops for Bonetto (32) and Carini (36) with their Maseratis.

Villoresi controlled the race from that point until the finish, including a new lap record, followed by Dorino Serafini and Clemar Bucci. Fangio achieved fourth place, which earned the admiration of the press for his spectacular comeback. Bucci achieved his best performance in international competitions.

The third race was held in Mar del Plata on The Torreon circuit. There were great expectations after a ferocious start, where Fangio got away first, followed by Ascari, Farina, Villoresi and González. After a few laps Villoresi overtook Ascari and Farina, and began to catch the leader. Then, on lap 13, on the climb to the Peralta Ramos Avenue, Villoresi tried to pass Fangio, but lost control and hit Fangio's car, and injured five spectators, thus ending the race for both drivers.

The crowd thought this had been a ploy of the Italian team to eliminate Fangio, and whistled with derision every time Ascari passed them. Even so, the Italian won the race, followed by Farina and Taruffi. After the race the relationship between the Italian and Argentinian press deteriorated and an incredible media battle ensued.

1950 – III Gran Premio Internacional Gral San Martín – Mar del Plata

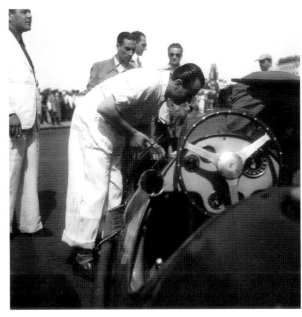

Far left: Froilán González' Maserati 4CLT before the start.

Left: Last touches before the race. Ferrari brought three official machines to Argentina, and a fourth car for the Argentine Automobile Club team.

Below: Ascari driving towards victory with the Ferrari at the Mar del Plata Circuit.

1950 Argentina – IV Copa de acción San Lorenzo – Rosario

The last race of the season was the San Lorenzo Cup which took place as a 60 lap event in the Independencia Park circuit at Rosario. Fangio achieved pole position and, after the chequered flag fell, he arrived at the first corner in the lead, followed by Ascari, Farina, Taruffi and Villoresi. Soon Villoresi took over third place and started chasing the leaders.

On lap 12, Ascari, who was then in second position, came into the pits with overheating problems, and left the race to Fangio, who then had a 28 second advantage. But on lap 17, when Fangio attempted to overtake Felice Bonetto, he risked a lot with the manoeuvre, suffered a series of spins and finally struck a lighting column which broke the car's steering, forcing him to abandon the race.

Fangio with the Ferrari 166 FL.

Fangio crashed his Ferrari against a lamp standard, breaking the car's steering. Members of the public dangerously invaded the circuit to try to help their idol; fortunately without any repercussions.

Benedict Campos, who had been in second place, overtook Villoresi on lap 30, to the delight of the spectators, who revived their hopes of seeing an Argentinian driver in the lead, but after a few more laps Campos suffered a full spin which relegated him to second place again. The race victory then went to Villoresi, followed by Campos and Farina.

Pit stop for Benedict Campos with the Ferrari 166FL of the Argentine team.

Defeat for the Mercedes-Benz W154

The Argentine Automobile Club had invested a large sum of money in sending the Argentine team to race in Europe for the 1950 season. So, to shrink the financial deficit, the ACA thought of organising two races, just days apart, in Buenos Aires for the International season. Without a suitable budget, many great drivers and teams from Europe could not participate, so only the official Mercedes-Benz 'works' team, one which had a special interest in promoting its cars in Argentina, was present.

The organisers did not want to use the Palermo circuit again, because of the previous racing deaths of Wimille and Pesatti, and elected to use a new circuit which had been designed and built alongside the metropolitan airport. This circuit included a long stretch of the North Costanera and with mixed park-type sections located between Avenida Sarmiento and Salguero Street, beside the Rio de la Plata.

The original plan was for a very fast track with two long straights. Fangio and González, who would run the Ferrari Automobile Club team, did not hesitate to criticise this, and advised the organisers to shorten the straights to lower the average speeds considering that, otherwise, the famous Mercedes W154 model had a significant difference in power in their favour. The circuit was modified, but, ironically, Fangio then received an invitation from the Mercedes team to run one of its three cars, and could not refuse since he had recently been appointed official dealer of the brand in Argentina. Karl Kling and Hermann Lang would be teammates.

1951 – Gran Premio Presidente Juan Domingo Perón – Costanera

The drivers before the race.

1951 – Gran Premio Presidente Juan Domingo Perón – Costanera

Karl Kling and Hermann Lang before the start.

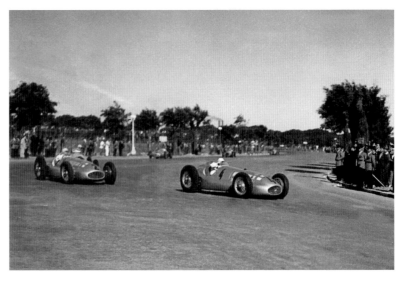

Lang and Fangio tackle a corner. This circuit had a low average speed, which balanced the difference between the powerful Mercedes models and the rest of the cars.

Froilán González about to overtake Lang. The supercharged two-litre Ferrari had 295 horsepower, while the Mercedes had 475bhp.

The ACA had also secured two Ferraris: one, with a short-wheelbase chassis, was for González to drive, and the longer wheelbase chassis would be for Oscar Gálvez. The supercharged two-litre Ferrari had 295 horsepower, while the Mercedes had 475bhp.

Fangio dominated the qualifying sessions, and no one doubted that he would win the race comfortably. However, González then surpassed all expectations, and, while the Mercedes failed during the race, this did not detract from a great performance by the 'Pampus Bull,' who circulated with great consistency.

González completed the 45 circuits in 1hr 35min 18sec, thereby winning the General Perón and the City of Buenos Aires Grand Prix in fine style. Hermann Lang finished second, 10.02 seconds behind, followed by Fangio, Oscar Gálvez, Alfredo Pian (Maserati) and Karl Kling.

The week between the first and second races was dominated by endless technical calculations. However, the fact that the Ferrari weighed 300kg less than the W154s, and

Hermann Lang with the W154. The Mercedes-Benz team had brought its own fuel, and used this throughout the race.

Fangio dominated the qualifying season, demonstrating his ability to adapt to any car.

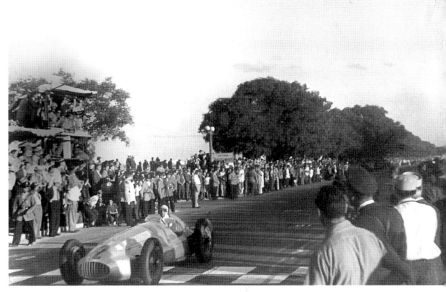

Fangio, with the Mercedes W154, finished in third place.

1951 – Gran Premio Maria Eva Duarte de Perón – Costanera

Sparkplug changes became routine for the Mercedes-Benz cars.

the shortening of the straights, made the 190bhp advantage held by Mercedes less important.

For the second race, the Mercedes were again on the front row, closely matched by González. After the first lap, Fangio's W154 was comfortably in the lead, followed by Lang and González. Fangio then broke all existing lap records, before having to make a pit stop, which cost him any chance he had. The same carburation failure as experienced in the previous race had happened again in this race, and could not be resolved despite several long-distance telephone calls to the German factory.

On the fifth lap, therefore, González took the lead, which he held until the end of the race. He did not only win because the more powerful Mercedes cars had several problems, but because he always drove with plenty of vigour and skill, and pushed his Ferrari to the limit without risking too much in search of victory.

The flag drops at the Costanera Norte of Buenos Aires circuit: the three Mercedes leave the line first.

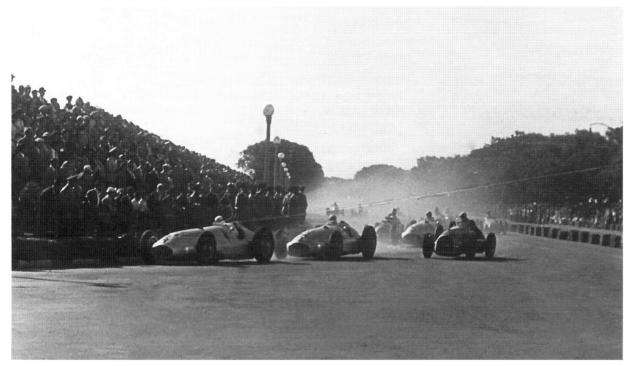

Also in the second race Fangio moved into first place, with González attacking outside him.

Kling and Lang in the first corner of the circuit Costanera.

In the second race Karl Kling made faster time than team-mate Lang, and finished in second place.

Froilán González finally beat all three Mercedes-Benz cars ... and got the win with the Ferrari 166FL.

1953

Ascari wins in a race marked by tragedy

The first-ever World Championship Formula 1 race to score points outside Europe was the Argentine Grand Prix of 1953, held on the new 17 de Octubre circuit in Buenos Aires. The race was for cars up to 2000cc and attracted a massive crowd of nearly 300,000 people, which sometimes overflowed onto the racetrack!

One of the pre-race expectations was to witness the return of Argentine hero Juan Manuel Fangio, who had remained mainly inactive throughout 1952, and, along with Froilán González, formed the Maserati team. News was the signing of the British driver Mike Hawthorn by Ferrari.

Alberto Ascari took the lead and held it until the end, for Fangio's and González' efforts to catch the race leader were unsuccessful. Despite taking a pit stop on lap 44 to change tyres, Ascari never lost the leading position.

1953 – I Gran Premio de la Republica Argentina

Above: Fangio appeared once again, after his Monza accident in 1952, with his six-cylinder Maserati.
Top right: The Englishman, Mike Hawthorn, before the race, with his Ferrari.
Bottom right: Ascari led from start to finish with his Ferrari in the first Formula 1 race ever held outside Europe.

Top left: Felice Bonetto with a Maserati A6GCM, which was abandoned on lap 32.
Top right: Race organiser Borgonova explains some features of the race under the watchful eyes of Manzon, Schell, Villoresi, Fangio, Schwelm-Cruz and Ascari.
Bottom right: The Ferrari team with four Ferrari 500s and the Maserati team with four A6GCMs. Ferraris were driven by Ascari, Farina and Villoresi, with a fourth car for its new signing, Mike Hawthorn. Maserati had the A6GCM chassis driven by Fangio, González, Bonetto and local hero Gálvez.

The 'Equipe Gordini' took part with five T16s for Jean Behra, Maurice Trintignant, Harry Schell, Robert Manzon and Carlos Menditeguy. The Gordinis weighed 540kg, and had six-cylinder engines developing 160hp at 6000rpm.

The truly sad note to this race was the terrible accident suffered by Jose Farina, whose car left the track and crashed into a crowd of spectators who had invaded the circuit when they found that the grandstands were completely full. Officially it was said that 19 people had been killed, and over 30 were injured.

Despite this tragedy, the race continued. Fangio had to retire because of differential problems in his Maserati, which left the second position to González until he also had to stop due to overheating problems. Finally, Villoresi crossed the finish line second, followed by González and Mike Hawthorn.

Continues on page 45

Drivers and machines lined up in front of the pit boxes, attentively listening to the anthems of competing countries.

Fangio, with a six-cylinder Maserati, retired with axle differential failure.

Villoresi, with his Ferrari, finished second. The Ferrari had four cylinders and an output of 190bhp at 6800rpm. The car weighed 610kg.

Alberto Ascari cruising towards victory with the Ferrari.

This study demonstrates the recklessness of the public. The Maserati of González is about to pass Bonetto, with many people standing on the edge of the track. The impending tragedy that took several lives was almost inevitable.

Fangio (2) about to overcome a Gordini and a Cooper-Bristol.

1953 – Gran Premio Ciudad de Buenos Aires

The Cooper Car Company made an official entry with cars for Alan Brown, John Barber and Adolfo Cruz. The Cooper Bristols had six-cylinder engines, which produced 130bhp, and a total weight of 508kg.

Froilán González with the two-litre supercharged Maserati.

Two weeks later, a Formula Libre race was promoted, to be used by the teams to test prototypes and solutions without breaking formula regulations, and then to use the successful developments in Formula 2 and Formula 1. On the very varied starting grid, therefore, was a variety of cars such as a GP Ferrari 2500 with supercharger, and a Ferrari 2000 without a supercharger, three old Alfa Romeos, a 4500 Talbot, two Maserati 4CLTs, and several assorted Gordinis and Coopers.

In qualifying for the Buenos Aires Grand Prix, this was clearly the domain of Ferrari over Maserati, when Ascari achieved the fastest time in his Ferrari 4500cc.

The race was then dominated by Ferrari, although Ascari withdrew the 375 after only a few laps. Other Ferraris, driven by Farina, Villoresi and Hawthorn, got podium places. González finished fourth, and was the only other car to stay on the same lap as the leaders.

Robert Manzon was the most prominent of the French Gordini team. At one point in the race he was second, but had to retire on lap 67.

Luigi Villoresi with his Ferrari.

Hawthorn finished fourth in his Ferrari debut.

Giuseppe Farina passed Villoresi on the eighth lap to take first place, and stayed there until the end of the race.

Giuseppe Farina gave a broadcast interview immediately after the victory.

Fangio, Trintignant, and the 1000km sports car race

The 1954 championship, marked the return of Formula 1, with cars having 2500cc engines. For the Argentina race, only Maserati could present a completely new car (the 250F), while the rest had adapted larger engines to fit in the existing chassis.

The great entertainers of previous seasons, like Alberto Ascari and Luigi Villoresi, could not come to race in 1954 because, at a late stage, they had left the Scuderia Ferrari team to join Lancia. Maserati presented six cars in Buenos Aires on this occasion, two experimental with De Dion rear suspension, and all equipped with 2500cc engines. Its drivers were Prince Bira and Luigi Musso, along with Fangio, Jorge Daponte, Mieres and Marimón.

Ferrari entered four official race cars for Mike Hawthorn, Giuseppe Farina and Umberto Maglioli, the fourth being given to Jose Froilán González, and painted in the traditional Argentinian colours of blue and yellow. The Gordini team, always modest and courageous, arrived at the Port of Buenos Aires with three cars, all based on Formula 2

1954 – II Gran Premio de la Republica Argentina

Maglioli, González, Marimón and Fangio talking before the start.

Just before the start with Farina (Ferrari 625) González (Ferrari 625) Fangio (Maserati 250F), and Hawthorn (Ferrari 625) at the front.

chassis, and with engines of 2500cc, with drivers Jean Behra, Ellie Bayol and Loyer.

For the race, the circuit known as 'Circuit Number 2,' 3.9km long, was employed, but laid out in an anti-clockwise direction because of the previous year's Farina accident. Early in the race it was the Ferraris that led, with Giuseppe Farina in the lead, more than six seconds ahead of Fangio. Everything then changed on lap 30 when a heavy rainstorm was unleashed.

The poor state of the track meant that it was completely flooded in some areas, which led to many spins and off-road excursions. On lap 60 Fangio came into the pits, where his team changed the tyres in 1min 15sec. However, this pit stop immediately generated a protest from the Ferrari team.

The initial move was made by Farina and Fangio, trying to get away from Mike Hawthorn, Onofre Marimón and De Graffenried. González remained on the start line.

Farina was in the lead of the race until lap 72, when he was overtaken by Fangio and, consequently, finished in second place.

Left: Louis Rosier with the blue-painted Ferrari 500.

The official Ferrari team working together. Umberto Maglioli with Ferrari 625 in front of Giuseppe Farina and Mike Hawthorn.

Froilán González chasing Fangio. The Ferrari was painted in blue and yellow – the Argentine motorsport colours.

Umberto Maglioli with the Ferrari 625 featured strongly in the first part of the race, chasing Hawthorn for the lead.

The Ferrari team manager Ugolini demanded the disqualification of the Argentine driver because he understood that during the operation more than the three authorised mechanics worked on the car. Actually an extra helper had reached in with a pair of goggles for Fangio to use in the rain.

With rain tyres fitted, Juan Manuel Fangio cut the deficit lap after lap to reduce the advantage that Farina had, and seven laps before the end he overtook the Italian, to win the first Formula 1 race of the year. Ferrari then claimed that Farina had allowed Fangio to pass because his pit crew had informed him that the Argentinian was already disqualified. That protest was not upheld, and Fangio won the first 8 points of the Championship.

Fangio receives the chequered flag in very wet conditions.

A week later, on a makeshift circuit in the General Paz Avenue, and on the Autódromo 17 de Octubre, the first 1000km was run in the City of Buenos Aires, with points for the World Sports Car Championship.

At the start there were ten Ferraris, six Jaguars, four Aston Martins, two Gordinis, two Cadillac-engined Allards, two Maseratis, six Porsches, one Borgward and one Osca, divided up into three classes: up to 1500cc, 1501cc to 3000cc, and 3001cc to 4500cc. Among the drivers were: Ninian Sanderson, Trintignant, Farina, Maglioli, Parnell, Salvadori, Collins, Griffith, Schell, Menditeguy, Ibáñez, Forrest Greene and the Marquis de Portago.

The race was comfortably won by the Farina-Maglioli pairing with a 4500cc Ferrari, followed by the three-litre Ferrari of Schell and De Portago, who were therefore first in their capacity class. Peter Collins and Pat Griffith, in an Aston Martin, finished third. The sad news of this event, however, was the death of Eric Forrest Greene after he overturned his Aston Martin on lap 23.

1954 – Buenos Aires 1000km

After the traditional Le Mans type start it was the Jaguar C-Type of Jimmy Stewart and Sanderson that was first off the line.

At the start there were ten Ferraris, six Jaguars, four Aston Martins, two Gordinis, two Cadillac-engined Allards, a Maserati, a Ford-engined Maserati, six Porsches, a Borgward and one Osca. Among the drivers, the most notable were Ninian Sanderson, Trintignant, Farina, Maglioli, Parnell, Salvadori, Collins, Griffith, Schell, Menditeguy, Ibáñez, Forrest Greene and the Marquis de Portago.

The Jaguar C-Type of Masten Gregory and Dale Duncan in a routine pit stop.

The splendour of the Jaguar C-Type as it leaves the pits.

The race was run on a mixed circuit integrating the Buenos Aires racetrack and the General Paz Avenue. Here is the winner, Giuseppe Farina, who ran with Maglioli with the Ferrari 375MM.

On January 31 the Grand Prix Formula Libre City of Buenos Aires race ran with virtually the same drivers who had competed two weeks before in the Formula 1 competition.

Twenty-one cars were entered, including the best exponents of the Fuerza Libre (free force) of the Mecánica Nacional (National Mechanics). In the race Maglioli led at first, but, after a few laps, he was passed by Mike Hawthorn, while Fangio had to retire from the event on the sixth lap with mechanical problems. Maurice Trintignant with the Ferrari 625 took over in second place after González retired.

The big surprise came on the very last lap when Hawthorn went off the road and broke his Ferrari's gearbox, leaving the race gifted to the French team running a similar machine, but one which was painted in the French motorsport national colour of blue. Roberto Mieres finished second, completing an excellent run in his A6GCM Maserati.

1954 – Gran Premio Ciudad de Buenos Aires

Drivers talking together before the start of the race.

Maurice Trintignant took victory in his blue-painted Ecurie Rosier Ferrari 625.

Seconds before the start, with four Ferraris on the front row – Farina, González, Hawthorn and Trintignant. The Englishman went off the track, and the car's engine stalled on the very last lap when he was in an easy lead, gifting victory to Trintignant.

The American Harry Schell ran an excellent race, and managed to finish in fourth place.

'Bitito' Mieres crosses the finish line to the delight of the public. In a great performance the Argentinian driver finished second with a Maserati A6GCM.

Juan Manuel Fangio and Mercedes-Benz – an excellent duo

1955 – III Gran Premio de la Republica Argentina

Fangio before the start of the event.

Stirling Moss heading to the track in his first race with Mercedes-Benz.

For this race there was an excellent turnout of Formula 1 cars. The Lancia team presented its spectacular D50 models with V8 engines, and a top class team of drivers in Alberto Ascari, Eugenio Castellotti and 'Gigi' Villoresi. The latest Ferraris had 265 horsepower engines, for Jose Froilán González, Maurice Trintignant and Giuseppe Farina. The biggest rivals of the two Italian teams were the eight-cylinder Mercedes-Benz W196s of Fangio, Karl Kling, Hans Herrmann and Stirling Moss. Maserati also entered several six-cylinder 250F cars for Behra, Menditeguy, Schell, Mieres, Musso, Bucci, Uria and Mantovani, while Gordini had machines for Élie Bayol, Pablo Birger and Jesus Ricardo Iglesias.

Early in the race Fangio started in the lead, followed by Ascari, Moss and González. Kling, Herrmann, Mieres and Schell formed the second group. A multiple accident between Birger, Menditeguy, Behra and Kling then eliminated them from the race.

On lap three Ascari passed into the lead, followed by González. In the first ten laps, however, the heat of the day began to affect some drivers, and Villoresi and Castelotti both dropped out. On lap 22 Ascari then went off the track, damaging his Lancia against a fence, and retired from the race, leaving González in the lead until lap 26, when he stopped and handed over his car to Farina because he had suffered heatstroke. Fangio was then in the lead until lap 35, when he made a 1min 20sec pit stop. Harry Schell then passed him, but stopped six laps later, and Mieres took over to catch the lead until he had to visit the pits. Fangio then took back the lead on lap 43, where he remained until the end of the race.

At the start Harry Schell with the Maserati 250F, Hans Herrmann with the Mercedes W196, and Eugenio Castellotti with a Lancia D50.

Juan Manuel Fangio's career was populated by a series of spectacular wins due to his driving ability, but here his physical strength enabled him to travel the entire race, even though there was a registered temperature of 55 degrees centigrade on the track surface! Only Fangio and Mieres could complete the course without rest or a change. In other teams the drivers had to alternate stints in the cars.

The second 1000km race had been proposed only a few months earlier, so several teams had no time to prepare their cars. Only Ferrari and Gordini were present with official teams. To populate the grid with cars, there were 30 Argentinian historic Turismo Carrera type cars.

The great candidate to win was the Ferrari 375 from the factory team, driven by the recent Le Mans race winners González and Trintignant. Maglioli/Bucci completed the team with a three-litre-engined car. The other drivers of these cars were the Argentine Enrique Díaz Sáenz Valiente and José María Ibáñez with the Ferrari 375 Plus, which had a five-litre engine.

In the first round, Kling, Birger and Menditeguy, with Maserati number 4 crashed into each other and ended up out of the race.

Ascari has just overtaken Fangio for the lead. In between is the Gordini T16 of the Argentine, Jesus Iglesias.

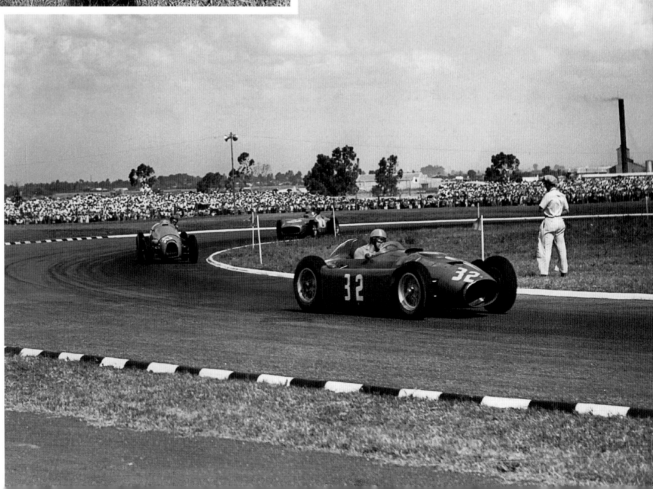

Eugenio Castellotti with the V8-engined Lancia D50. The Italian drove well, but suffered from the intense heat, so had to stop several times to cool off.

Fangio at speed with the Mercedes-Benz W196. The Argentinian did not obey the order of team-manager Neubauer to stop to cool off, and continued to the end to win the race.

Alberto Ascari was in the lead with the Lancia D50 until he retired on lap 21.

Karl Kling with the Mercedes-Benz W196 in Saturday practice. On race day he crashed in the very first corner.

From the start Trintignant took the lead, but Sáenz Valiente then overtook him and came past the pits in the lead on the first lap. When the first driver changes took place on lap seven, González was approaching the lead, but the fuel pump on his engine broke, and the car was forced out of the race. Without pressure, the five-litre Ferrari of Sáenz Valiente and Ibáñez scored a comfortable win, while Najurieta/Rivero were second in a 4.5-litre Ferrari.

1955 Argentina – Buenos Aires 1000km

Start of the 1000km which qualified for points for the World Manufacturers' Championship. Trintignant, with the Ferrari 118LM, left the line first, followed by the Allard J2X (with Cadillac engine) of Franco Bruno and the Ferrari 375 of Sáenz Valiente, who, along with Jose Maria Ibañez, won the race.

Fangio crosses the line and gets the first points in the quest for a new F1 world title.

Sáenz Valiente's 375 Plus Ferrari on its way to victory.

The Gordini T24S of Élie Bayol and Harry Schell took fifth place. The Touring Category was won by Oscar Gálvez in a Ford V8.

On January 30, a race was held on the Number 4 circuit, called the Grand Prix of Buenos Aires, under the rules of Formula Libre, so that the teams could use the event to test their new developments before the European season. The race was run in two sections of 30 laps, the final classification being the sum of both partial times. The entry was almost the same as earlier, with the cars and drivers that had started the Formula 1 race run a fortnight beforehand, except that the Lancia team had already returned to Italy, because it did not have any larger engines to use.

Mercedes took the opportunity to test the engines that the 300 SLR would be using in future sport races in the 300SLRs, and ran three W196 single-seaters equipped with three-litre engines. Ferrari meanwhile, prepared a 625 with a three-litre engine. Maserati had two 2.7-litre engines mounted in 250Fs driven by Schell and Behra.

At the start, Moss took the lead, followed by Fangio and Kling. However, as the laps unfolded, Farina's Ferrari began attacking, overtaking the Mercedes-Benz cars one by one, and finally took the lead. Fangio then overtook Moss and did the same with Farina, but he could not beat the Italian, who finally managed to overcome the Argentinian, and therefore took victory in the first heat.

1955 Argentina – Gran Premio Ciudad de Buenos Aires

A few minutes before the start of the first heat – González (12), Trintignant (14), and Fangio (2) on the front row.

Behra and Mantovani with the Maserati 250Fs of the Officine Alfieri Maserati team. Behind is the Ferrari 625 of Clemar Bucci. The race was 'Formula Libre' and the teams took the opportunity to test their new developments before the European season.

Jean Behra in his Maserati 250F.

In the background, Fangio's Mercedes-Benz W196 (2) on pole is closest to Trintingnant's Ferrari 625 (14) and the blue and yellow Ferrari 625 of Froilán González (12). In the centre of the picture is Jean Behra's Maserati 250F.
(Copyright @jarrotts.com)

Farina driving this Ferrari 625 overtook Moss and Fangio to win the first heat.

Following the second start, Fangio took the lead, but quickly it was Moss that went to the front. Farina's Ferrari was hit by Birger's Gordini and, after the collision, the engine stopped and the car had to retire from the race. Moss controlled this heat, but did not cancel out the advantage that Fangio had taken in the first event. Accordingly, Moss won the heat, followed by Fangio and Trintingnant. Overall, though, Fangio won the race ahead of Moss by almost 12 seconds, and was ahead of González/Trintingnant by more than 30 seconds.

Fangio followed by Stirling Moss. The Argentine won the two-heat race, and was ahead of Moss by nearly 12 seconds. The Mercedes, with a specially-shaped bonnet panel, used this race to test the three-litre engines which would equip the 300 SLR racing sports car.

1956

Fangio vs Moss

Argentina was again the setting for the first F1 race of the 1956 season. The rejigged Lancia-Ferrari team was made up of the reigning F1 champion, Juan Manuel Fangio, Belgium's Olivier Gendebien, Britain's Peter Collins and the two Italians Luigi Musso and Eugenio Castellotti. Maserati rivals were driven by none other than the British drivers Stirling Moss and Mike Hawthorn, Frenchman Jean Behra and Argentines Carlos Menditeguy and Froilán González.

1956 – IV Gran Premio de la Republica Argentina

The Officine Alfieri Maserati team presented six Maserati 250Fs for Stirling Moss, Jean Behra, Carlos Menditeguy, Chico Landi, Froilán González and Luigi Piotti.

After practice ended, the Lancia Ferrari D50 was ahead of the Maserati. Fangio set the fastest time on the Saturday, but then had to swap the Lancia's engine, and the car did not work as well as it had before.

In the race Fangio made several pit stops to try to fix the flaws in his car's engine, so by lap 18 had already lost four places relative to the leader, who at that point was Menditeguy, followed by Moss.

The Ferrari team then decided to ask Luigi Musso to hand over his car to Fangio. When the Argentine returned to the track with the new machine he found himself in fifth place almost one lap behind the leader, Menditeguy, who was

The Brazilian Chico Landi with the Maserati 250F of the Officine Alfieri Maserati team at the pits. He finished fourth, sharing his car with Italian Gerino Gerini, to become the first Brazilian driver to score points in Formula 1 when 47 years old.

Mike Hawthorn took an excellent third place in the final standings with his Maserati 250F, owned by the Owen Racing Motor Association Team, and equipped with wheels and disc brakes by Dunlop.

running strongly and with a lead of 30 seconds over Moss, but he then spun off against a fence and ended up having to abandon the chase.

At the mid-race point Moss was well in the lead, 55 seconds ahead of Fangio, but he was cutting two seconds per lap to the delight of the crowd, and after a demonstration of impeccable handling found himself in the lead. Moss dropped out a few laps later, and Jean Behra took his place.

On lap 28, Fangio then spun out, yet managed to return to the track with the help of the marshals. Maserati technical director, Nello Ugolini, then filed a protest for that reason against the leader, but the FIA, after analysing the manoeuvre, dismissed the claim.

Continues on page 77

Eugenio Castellotti had to retire from the race due to the Ferrari's gearbox problems.

The Maserati 250F of Luigi Piotti, which had more power than the previous year, and some improvements in aerodynamics and suspension.

Left to right: Peter Collins, Luigi Musso and Eugenio Castellotti before the start.

Moss was in front in his Maserati, until lap 80 when he was overtaken by Fangio, and one lap later had to abandon the race with engine trouble.

Landi, the Uruguayans González and Uria, Menditeguy, Hawthorn and Moss in the pre-race meeting.

Fangio finalising details in his car before the start. The race ended with controversy when Maserati protested the result, arguing that Fangio had received a push-start after his spin. The protest – and a later appeal – were both dismissed.

The Lancia-Ferraris were dominant in qualifying with Fangio (30), Castellotti (32) and Musso on the front row of the grid, joined by Behra. González, Menditeguy (6) and Moss on row two, while Hawthorn, Collins, Olivier Gendebien (38 with the Ferrari 555) and Chico Landi (10) were on the third row.

The first few metres of the race with Musso first, followed by González, Castellotti and Menditeguy.

Fangio chasing Menditeguy with the Maserati, who had a lead of 30 seconds, but just when he seemed to be a sure winner, he spun off the road and had to retire.

Froilán González at speed with the Maserati 250F. He retired on lap 24 with engine problems.

Since Juan Manuel Fangio was the leader, and maintained this to the end, no change was then recorded in the placings. Jean Behra seemed as though he might overtake Fangio, because the French driver made up valuable seconds over the leader, lap after lap, but then spun off, and lost all chance of winning, so stopped pressing, and maintained his second place ahead of Mike Hawthorn.

Right: Fangio on his way to victory in Musso's car. The Argentine had to stop in the pits on lap 23 with mechanical failure, so the Ferrari team boss signalled Luigi Musso to hand over his machine to the World Champion, and to let him claim the victory.

Fangio won 5 points for first position and for his lap record time. Musso scored another 4 points of the 8 that were distributed for the top spot.

On January 29th, the Buenos Aires 1000km race for sports cars attracted a 32-car entry. The main contenders, who might win, were the six-cylinder Maserati 300S cars of the official factory team, driven by Moss/Behra and Menditeguy/Froilán González, or the five-litre Ferraris of Fangio/Castellotti and Musso/Collins.

The first part of the race was a struggle between Fangio, Moss and Musso. Then came the change over 'relays,' but as Moss did not stop he was therefore ahead of Castellotti. Halfway into the race, Moss handed over his car to Menditeguy, while the Fangio and Castellotti Ferrari needed a pit stop to make repairs, after the Italian had run over a dog. On lap 70 Castellotti was again replaced by Fangio, who, after a spectacular comeback drive, found himself on the same lap as the race leader. But then, with only 15 laps to go, Fangio was forced out, due to mechanical problems.

A Le Mans-type start.

1956 – 1000km Buenos Aires

Fangio and Castellotti shared a Ferrari 410 Plus.

Luigi Musso and Peter Collins with the Ferrari 410 Sport of the Scuderia Ferrari.

Finally, the race was won by the Maserati of Moss/ Mphasisenditeguy followed by the Ferrari of Gendebien/Hill.

A few weeks later the City of Buenos Aires Prix, a Formula Libre event, was run on the San Martin circuit in the city of Mendoza. In the race, Fangio was first off the line, and arrived in the lead at the first corner, followed by Castellotti and Musso. These positions were maintained until Castellotti and Musso both had to retire, with a crash and a broken radiator respectively.

Moss was running second in his Maserati 250F and was trying to overtake Fangio, but then spun, and definitely lost all chance of taking the lead. Fangio won the race followed by Moss. Behra was ranked third and the other Maserati driver, Menditeguy, was fourth.

Top left: Peter Collins in one of the main avenues of Buenos Aires.
Bottom left: Francisco Landi and Gerino Gerini with the Maserati 300S of the Officine Alfieri Maserati team.
Below: Froilán González at speed with the Maserati 300S.

1957

Italian rules

The first of three scheduled races for the 1957 season qualified for the Drivers' World Championship. Fangio had moved from Ferrari to Maserati to team up with Moss, Behra, Harry Schell and Carlos Menditeguy, all in 250F models. Peter Collins, Mike Hawthorn, Luigi Musso, Maurice Trintignant, Césare Perdisa, Eugenio Castellotti, Alfonso de Portago and Wolfgang Von Trips all figured in Ferraris.

1957 – V Gran Premio de la Republica Argentina

Stirling Moss was fastest in qualifying, beating Fangio and Jean Behra, all with Maserati 250Fs. Castellotti completed the front row with the Ferrari. Closest to the camera, with older Maseratis, were Menditeguy (8) and Schell (22).

In addition, there were Scuderia Centro-Sud cars for Harry Schell and Giorgio Scarlatti; Joaquin Bonnier had two 1956-model Maseratis; there was a two-litre Ferrari for Alessandro de Tomaso, and Luigi Piotti completed the field with a Maserati.

On the Saturday, Moss took pole position, closely followed by Fangio, but when the race started the British driver was stuck on the grid with throttle linkage problems. Behra then jumped into first place, followed by Castellotti and Fangio. Coming up fast, Castellotti took the lead on lap three, but was displaced on the ninth by Behra, who in turn lost it to

Collins. Then problems with the Ferraris began around the 13th lap. First, it was Collins on lap 25 with transmission problems that could not be solved. Five laps later, both Hawthorn and Musso had to stop with the same problems. Only Castellotti managed to stay in the race.

With a quarter of the race completed, Fangio took the lead, attacked by Behra, with third held by Castellotti. Only ten laps before the end the two leading Maseratis both stopped in the pits to refuel, and Fangio went ahead, winning the race, demonstrating the clear superiority of the Maserati.

Continues on page 86

Jean Behra with a Maserati 250F (6) and Mike Hawthorn with Lancia-Ferrari 801 (16), waiting for the chequered flag.

Fangio in the lead in the Maserati, followed by the Ferraris of Hawthorn and Wolfgang von Trips, in the early laps of the race.

Collins with the Lancia Ferrari 801. The Prancing Horse cars had V8 engines and new chassis developments.

Menditeguy finished third, producing his best-ever result in Grand Prix.

Eugenio Castellotti, at speed. It would be Castellotti's last Grand Prix. He was killed testing a Ferrari at Modena two months later.

Mike Hawthorn in his Ferrari. In the early laps of the race the Prancing Horse cars made good progress, but then began to lose ground due to transmission failures.

Fangio and Behra reach the finishing line to the delight of the public. The race showed the great superiority of the latest Maserati.

Awards for the winners.

For the 1000km event, in contrast to the previous year, the Automobile Club Argentino had decided to promote the race on a 'park type' circuit to the north of Buenos Aires.

European teams were very unhappy with the new layout, but after the organisers had received approval from the FIA in Paris, they decided to compete in the race.

1957 – 1000km Buenos Aires

Ron Flockhart crashed the Jaguar D-Type in Saturday practice, and could not start the race.

Top left: Stirling Moss took pole position with the Maserati.
Top right: Castellotti before the start.
Right: The start, with Moss' Maserati 450S (2) on pole, sharing the first row with the Ferrari 290S of Castellotti (4) and the Ferrar (1), hidden by the starter.

The novelty of the race was the presence of the Ecurie Ecosse team with two D-type Jaguars, to be driven by Flockhart, Sanderson and the Argentine Mieres. For Maserati there were Fangio, Moss and Menditeguy, sharing a 450S and a 300S model. Ferrari competed with Collins, Hawthorn, Castellotti, De Portago, Masten Gregory and Luigi Musso, with two 290MMs and two 290S models.

After the chequered flag dropped, Moss sprinted out first followed by all the Ferraris. Castellotti made a first lap pit stop with problems in the car's differential. At the end of the third lap Collins and Musso also had to stop with gearbox problems. After 15 laps Moss was in the lead, followed by Gregory, De Portago, Behra and Sanderson.

On lap 24 Moss handed over the wheel to Fangio, who held on to the pace and increased the lead, but on lap 56 the

The pits of what was a very dangerous circuit.

Moss at the wheel of the Maserati 450S of the Officine Alfieri Maserati Team. In concert with Fangio, the pair dominated the first part of the race, before retiring on lap 58.

The Scuderia Madunina Brazil Maserati A6GC leaving the pits.

Detail work being carried out on this Ferrari just before the start.

Maserati had to return to the pits with insoluble differential problems, which forced it to retire.

Following the withdrawal of the leading Maserati, the Ferraris driven by Gregory, Perdisa, Castellotti and Musso took over in the leading positions. Moss took over the wheel of the Behra/Menditeguy Maserati, which was in third place, and began chasing the leaders, soon reaching and passing Castellotti into second place, but not able to reach the top spot. Eventually, the winner was the 3.5-litre Ferrari of Gregory/Castellotti/Musso. The Jaguar D-Type of Sanderson/Mieres was placed fourth, three laps down.

The close of the 1957 season came with the Buenos Aires Grand Prix, which was a Formula Libre race, and run in two heats of 30 laps each, the final result being the total of times on both races. It was held on Circuit Number 2 of the 17 de Octubre racetrack. *Continues on page 92*

Roberto Mieres with the Jaguar D-type of the Ecurie Ecosse.

Opposite:
Top left: Ninian Sanderson and Roberto Mieres finished in fourth place with the Jaguar D-type.
Top right: The Porsche 550 RS with Curt Delfosse in the pits.
Bottom: Fangio with the Maserati 450S on the main straight of the Costanera Circuit.

1957 – XI Gran Premio Ciudad de Buenos Aires

Right: Moss with the Maserati 250F was unable to start the second heat because of a mechanical problem.

In the second race of the season (an event which carried no points for the World Championship), Juan Manuel Fangio won comfortably with his Maserati.

At the time of the race the ambient temperature was very high. Castellotti took the lead, followed closely by Hawthorn, Fangio, Moss and Behra. In the middle of the race Fangio then made progress, and, helped by Behra, began to pull away, winning the first heat by 26 seconds over Behra, then Hawthorn and Castellotti.

The heat had affected the drivers so much that some had to be assisted to get out of their cockpits. Hawthorn overcame Castellotti a few metres after the start of the second race. Fangio was at that point in second place, and seemed to decide to take care of the car, and to preserve the advantage obtained in the first of the two heats. Then, on lap 15 everything changed, to the great excitement of the crowd: the Argentine closed in on, then overtook Hawthorn. A few laps later, however, Fangio gave way to Behra, but no one could match Peter Collins, who overtook Hawthorn, Fangio and Behra to win the heat. Accordingly, Fangio won the two-part race followed by Behra, Musso and Collins.

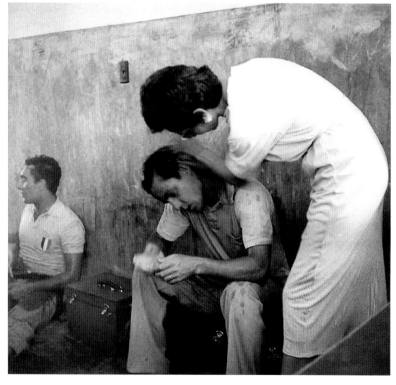

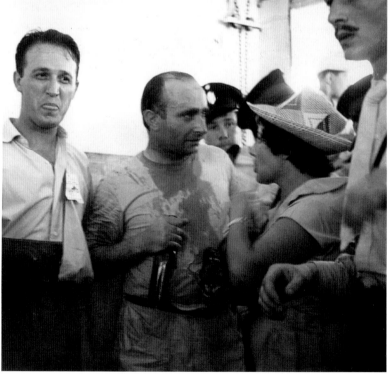

Jean Behra put in an excellent performance and finished second in both races.

Opposite:
Far left: With almost 55°C/131°F recorded at the track, the heat seriously affected the drivers, and some had to be assisted.
The Ferrari drivers Masten Gregory and Musso are seen here, trying to recover.
Left, top and bottom: Mike Hawthorn, Castellotti, von Trips and Fangio all freshen up at the pits.

1958

First win for a rear-engined car

Uncertainty surrounding the actual running of the first race of 1958 in Buenos Aires meant that the British teams were largely absent. A total of just ten cars reached the starting line of the race – this being a low point in the history of Formula 1. Ferrari and Maserati, plus a special Cooper-Coventry-Climax, were the only teams to show up. For all these reasons, the other teams – Lotus, Vanwall and BRM – asked that the race should score no points for the Championship.

Ferrari entered its official team with Luigi Musso, Peter Collins and Mike Hawthorn, all in the latest 246 model. Maserati handed over responsibility to the Scuderia American where the cars were driven by Juan Manuel Fangio, Jean Behra, Carlos Menditeguy, Harry Schell, Paco Godia and H Gould, all of them in 250F models.

1958 – VI Gran Premio de la Republica Argentina

The Maseratis arrive at the circuit. The SudAmerican Scuderia was comprised of Juan Manuel Fangio, Jean Behra, Carlos Menditeguy, Harry Schell, Paco Godia and H Gould.

The Maserati 250F waiting for action.

Moss' victory with a Cooper T43 Climax was the first F1 win for a rear-engined car. (Copyright @jarrotts.com)

Fangio set the fastest times, and claimed pole position, but it took too long to change tyres and he lost his chance. He finished in fourth place.

In the meantime, Stirling Moss had asked Rob Walker to send a Cooper to race in the Grand Prix. This tiny car caused great curiosity, and the general opinion was that it stood little chance of victory against the powerful Italian teams.

This opinion seemed to be confirmed after the start, because Fangio established a comfortable lead at once, taking a great advantage over the rest of the field. Peter Collins' car suffered a broken axle shaft, which caused its retirement on the first lap.

Until lap 30, there had been no more surprises – except the remarkable progress of Moss' Cooper into second

Fangio (2), with the Maserati, was fastest in practice with Hawthorn (20), Collins (18) both in Ferraris, and Behra (4) with another Maserati all alongside him on the front row of the grid. Musso, Menditeguy and Moss shared row two. Moss' Cooper (14) looked tiny in this company. (Copyright @jarrotts.com)

Behra in his Maserati 250F shot into the lead, followed by Hawthorn with a Ferrari Dino 246, Fangio (Maserati 250F) and Moss with his Cooper T43-Climax. Peter Collins was forced out just metres later with a driveshaft failure. (Copyright @jarrotts.com)

Menditeguy, with his Maserati 250F, spun in front of Hawthorn, who could not avoid him, and drove into the back of the number 6.

place behind Fangio, with Behra and Hawthorn behind him. Then on lap 35 Fangio had to make a pit stop to change tyres, losing the lead, and 36 seconds which could not be recovered. By then Moss was already in the front with his incredible little car.

In the last 10 laps Moss, whose car had badly-worn tyres, juggled with a 30-second lead over Musso, who was ordered to attack Moss, but this instruction came too late and Musso never caught up with the Cooper. Moss managed to win,

creating a landmark in automotive history, as this was the very first F1 victory for a rear-engined car.

The second race of the season was the Buenos Aires 1000km event, which was valid for the 1958 World Sports Car Championship of Makes, and would return to the traditional layout of the Autodromo of Buenos Aires and Gral Paz Avenue.

In this race there were three rival makes – the traditional Ferrari and Maserati combatants, and the German Porsches.

Continues on page 102

Moss' Cooper had problems with the gearbox at the start of the race, but then overcame Hawthorn, Behra and Fangio to win.

Opposite:
Top: Hawthorn at speed with the Ferrari V6. He took third place.
Bottom: Moss in Rob Walker's Cooper-Climax 43 on the way to victory. No one would have predicted a victory for Cooper, with half a litre engine capacity deficit, and 100hp less than the rest of the cars.

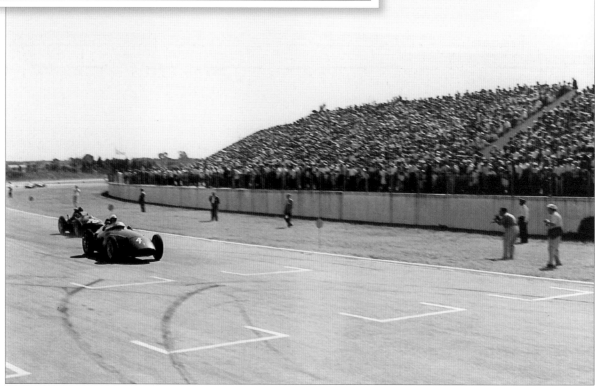

Behra and Hawthorn on the main straight.

Moss carried by the public after the win as if he was Fangio. The little Cooper's triumph remained in the memory of the more than 100,000 spectators present at the autodrome.

The Ferraris were the Testarossas with V12 2953cc engines, with a single overhead camshaft layout and 300hp. The Maserati cars provided by the Scuderia Centro Sud were the 300S models, reserved for Juan Manuel Fangio and Stirling Moss, who were former Grand Prix rivals. Moss, however, after testing the Maserati and breaking the engine, decided to ride along with Jean Behra in an official 1.6-litre Porsche which had a 140 horsepower engine.

Although Ferrari monopolised the top positions from the beginning (Collins, von Trips and Neumann), Fangio and his Maserati then began to fight, and he was behind the leaders in the second lap. Then, on the third lap, Fangio suffered a slide, went off the track, and smashed the front of the car into a fence. Fangio had to stop for his crew to make repairs, but did manage to get back on track after a delay. With this, the Ferraris then occupied the two top positions. The Collins/Hill team kept up the leadership until the end of the race, with von Trips/Hawthorn holding second until they were overtaken by Moss' Porsche.

Even so, on lap 55 the Ferrari's straight-line speed was too strong for the Porsche. The Porsche finally scored a brilliant third place. The Venezuelan couple of Drogo and González finished fourth in a white Ferrari Testarossa.

On Sunday, 2 February, the City of Buenos Aires Grand Prix was run to Formule Libre rules, making it the only significant race in the world, at that time, where teams could enter all engine sizes and all models.

This was seriously criticised because of the very noticeable difference in the performance between some of the cars, which it was thought might cause major problems.

1958 – 1000km de Buenos Aires

The Scuderia Ferrari entered three 250 TRs, driven by Collins/P Hill, Musso/Hawthorn and Gendebien/von Trips. The Scuderia Centro Sud entered two 300S types, one of which had been reserved for Juan Manuel Fangio and another for Moss. Even so, Moss, after testing the Maserati, decided instead to drive the Porsche 550 RS with Jean Behra.

Top left: The winner, Peter Collins, with the Ferrari 250 TR58, overtaking the Ferrari 750 Monza of Celso Lara/Barberis on the General Paz Avenue.
Bottom left: Fangio, with the Maserati 300S, suffered a slide and smashed the front of his car, and was forced to retire.
Above: Moss, after testing the Maserati 300S and breaking the engine, decided to jump in the Porsche 1600 and share it with Jean Behra, and obtained a brilliant victory in the 1500cc class, and third place in the general classification.

Wolfgang von Trips (Ferrari 250 Testarossa) in the pits.

In the end there were 13 GP cars in the race. Fangio, Carlos Menditeguy, Jean Behra, Joakim Bonnier, Horace Gould, Roberto Mieres, Roberto Bonomi and Kent Kavanagh all drove Maseratis. With Ferrari were Mike Hawthorn, Peter Collins, Luigi Musso and Wolfgang von Trips. Stirling Moss arrived with the two-litre Cooper-Climax that had brought him to victory only two weeks earlier, with the opening of the World F1 Championship. Mecánica Nacional entries were: Jose Froilán González in a Ferrari with Chevrolet engine, Jesus Ricardo Iglesias with a Chevrolet, Ramón Requejo with a Chevrolet, and the Uruguayans Marcos Galvan (with a Ford) and Danton Bazet and Asdrubal Fontes Bayardo, both with Chevrolets.

1958 – XIV Gran Premio Ciudad de Buenos Aires

Hawthorn with his V6 Ferrari in the paddock. He won the first heat but broke a driveshaft at the start of heat 2. (Copyright @jarrotts.com)

The Maserati 250Fs of Juan Manuel Fangio, Jean Behra and Carlos Menditeguy. (Copyright @jarrotts.com)

The cars heading for the starting grid.
(Copyright @jarrotts.com)

Fangio before the start of the 14th edition of the Grand Prix of Buenos Aires. It was the last race won by the Argentine driver.
(Copyright @jarrotts.com)

The race was run in two heats of 30 laps each, with the winner declared by the best aggregate time. The first session was run in persistant rain, and as the cars went into the first corner after the start, a clash between Iglesias and Moss put both drivers out of the race, while Fangio and Hawthorn went ahead in the lead. Hawthorn withstood pressure from Fangio for 30 laps, and acheived a fine victory in his Ferrari.

In the second heat Hawthorn was left at the start, and conceded the lead to Fangio, who retained his advantage over Musso. The Italian then had some problems in the last stages and was overtaken by Menditeguy, who finished second.

Aggregating the times for both heats gave victory to Fangio, and so the Argentinian won his last race before he retired from racing in the Reims Grand Prix in June 1958.

The cars were lined up on the grid when it was noticed that Menditeguy and Behra were missing. Fangio, Moss and Collins asked the stewards to delay the start for 15 minutes. In fact, they allowed only five minutes, and the race was then started without the missing pair. (Copyright @jarrotts.com)

Menditeguy's 250F overtaking the Uruguayan Marcos Galvan in a Ford Special.

Peter Collins broke the axle shaft of his Ferrari Dino 246 at the start and had to retire.

The start of the first heat. The race was for Formula 1 cars and those of the Mecánica Nacional. This decision was criticised because of the noticeable difference in performance.

1960

British rule

For Argentina's return to the Formula 1 calendar after a year's absence, all the very best cars and drivers were present. Cooper presented five T51 cars with Coventry-Climax engines for Moss, Brabham, McLaren, Trintignant and Schell and two with four-cylinder Maserati engines for the Argentines Bonomi and Menditeguy. BRM entered two P25s for Bonnier and Graham Hill. Innes Ireland drove a Lotus Climax Type 18 and there were three new Ferrari D246s for Allison, von Trips, Phil Hill and Froilán González. To complete the grid there were several Maserati 250s and one Behra-Porsche for Masten Gregory.

Stirling Moss took pole with the Cooper-Climax; however, when the flag fell, it was Innes Ireland who took the lead in his Lotus, although he then spun off the track a few metres later – without hitting anyone, or damaging his car, but leaving the lead to Bonnier, followed by Graham Hill and Moss.

1960 – VI Gran Premio de la Republica Argentina

Jack Brabham and Juan Manuel Fangio shake hands before the start.

Graham Hill, in the BRM, fought for second place for several laps in an emotional duel with Stirling Moss.

The winner, Bruce McLaren, at age 23, was the youngest driver in the race.

Stirling Moss was on pole in the Cooper-Climax; Innes Ireland with a Lotus and the BRMs of Hill and Jo Bonnier were alongside. When the flag fell, Innes Ireland was first away.

Moss soon overtook the two leading BRMs, but in mid-race his car suffered from suspension problems, so Bonnier's BRM regained the lead, now closely followed by Ireland in the Lotus.

Bonnier had to stop with engine trouble and lost the race; that was when Ireland appeared in the lead, but then the Lotus began to experience gearbox problems. The Ferraris never influenced the development of the race, and Jack Brabham had to retire because of a fault in the transmission of his Cooper-Climax.

The delay of Bonnier and Ireland then switched the spotlight to Bruce McLaren. The New Zealander took the lead with 12 laps to go, after making eight overtaking manoeuvres in the race. Allison came in second with the Ferrari. Moss took over Trintignant's car and came in third.

After one lap, the Lotus of Innes Ireland led the pack, followed by Bonnier. Behind were Graham Hill, Phil Hill, Froilán González, Jack Brabham and Menditeguy.

Bonnier had to get out of the car to cool off. He led the first part of the race.

Innes Ireland, with the Lotus Climax 18, chasing the Cooper Climax T51 of Jack Brabham.

Twenty-eight cars were officially registered for the 1000km race, run under new FIA regulations which required all cars to have windscreens, a luggage container to accept a suitcase, and doors with certain minimum measurements.

The most novel of all the cars was the Maserati 'Birdcage' of the Camoradi American team, which had a four-cylinder 2000cc chassis, made up of a multitude of small-diameter steel tubes; this driven by Gurney and Gregory. Ferrari presented two models of the new 250 TR type for Phil Hill/Allison and von Trips/Ginther along with one 246 Dino with a 2400cc V6 engine, to be driven by Froilán González and Scarfiotti. Porsche was allowed to run at the last moment, even though its cars did not meet all the new rules. There

were three RSK 718s for Bonnier/Graham Hill, Trintignant/Hermann and Gendebien/Barth.

In the race it was Dan Gurney who took the lead immediately, followed by the Ferrari of Allison and Ginther, which was trying valiantly trying to keep pace with the new Maserati.

Gurney beat all the lap records, lap after lap, but, nearly three hours into the race, the Maserati's gearbox began to fail, and the car had to be retired on lap 57, which left race victory to Ferrari.

After more than six hours of racing, only 11 of the 23 starters finished. Once again it was Phil Hill and his Ferrari who won the race – as he had done two years earlier –

Continues on page 116

1960 – 1000km de Buenos Aires

The 3000cc V12 Ferraris of Phil Hill/Cliff Allison and Wolfgang von Trips/Richie Ginther dominated the second half of the race after the American Maserati team's retirement.

The drivers sprint to their cars, with Richie Ginther, Ludovico Scarfiotti and Celso Lara Barberis reaching theirs first. The race was won by Phil Hill with Cliff Allison, in a Ferrari 250 Testa Rossa. (Courtesy jarrotts.com)

Dan Gurney with the Birdcage Maserati of the Camoradi American team.

Jo Bonnier and Graham Hill finished in third place with the Porsche 718 RSK.

The Ferrari 250GT of Venezuelans Ugo Tosa and Silvano Turco on the main straight of the racetrack.

though this time with Cliff Allison as his team-mate. It was the second car from Scuderia Ferrari (driven by von Trips and Ginther) which took second place, while Jo Bonnier and

Graham Hill came third (and first in the 1600cc class) with the Porsche. Fourth, with a great performance, came the Brazilian team of Barberis/Heins in their old Maserati 300S.

1960 – XIII Buenos Aires Grand Prix – Córdoba

The BRM P25.

On Saturday, during practice and qualifying, Juan Manuel Fangio did some laps in the Porsche built by the late Jean Behra.

On February 14th, on a 3.1km circuit, the Buenos Aires Grand Prix was held in the Sarmiento 'park type' Circuit in the city of Córdoba.

On Saturday Fangio accepted an invitation to drive Ettore Chimeri's Maserati, but almost fell into a deep ravine, after the car unexpectedly skidded and left the circuit.

Even though it had originally signed a contract to compete in

Brabham and McLaren in the Cooper Climax cars, ahead in the first stages of the race, followed by Menditeguy, Trintignant and Bonnier.

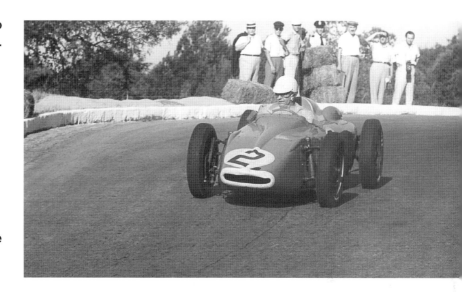

Jack Brabham, with the Cooper, has overtaken Gino Munaron in the Maserati 250F.

Maurice Trintignant passes Dan Gurney with the BRM for first place and heads towards victory.

all three races, Ferrari did not appear with its cars in this race. Enzo Ferrari, it seems, had ordered the return of the cars to Europe after their poor performance in the Argentine Grand Prix. Neither did Stirling Moss show up to race.

Another curious incident was the non-appearance of the BRM truck, to the great concern of the mechanics who needed to work on the cars after the race in Buenos Aires. In the end it arrived on the Saturday, when practice had already begun, and with several parts missing. The truck arrived with a drunk driver, but somehow the English mechanics did their best to present the car.

On race day the temperature was 38 degrees centigrade. Australian Jack Brabham got away first, followed by his team-mate, Bruce McLaren, then Maurice Trintignant also in a Cooper, and Dan Gurney in the BRM: McLaren dropped out a few laps later, when the engine oil cooler broke up. A similar fate also swept away Brabham, with a malfunction in the fuel pump. Dan Gurney then went into the lead, closely shadowed by the Swedish driver, Joakim Bonnier, in the other BRM.

Innes Ireland with the Lotus 16 Climax of the Team Lotus equipe. He retired on lap 68.

Dan Gurney finished in second place, despite having to manage the final laps with only the top gear working.

Bruce McLaren was the first to abandon the race after going off track and breaking the engine's oil cooler.

Carlos Menditeguy ran an excellent race in the Cooper with a Maserati engine.

At mid-race the BRMs began to fail, Bonnier with oil pressure problems and Gurney with gearbox problems, which allowed Trintignant to take the lead. Menditeguy with a Cooper Maserati achieved third place, to the delight of the public, but he retired a few laps later.

The fight for victory then focused between Gurney and Trintignant, who battled for the lead until lap 64, after which the Frenchman, with superb driving, got away from Gurney and took the victory. The Italian Gino Munaron was the third to finish – remarkable because he had started in last place in an ageing Maserati.

This race, though, came at the end of the season – and the golden age of Argentine motoring was over …

British driver Alan Stacey with his Lotus 16 Climax.

The traditional Formula Libre event which closed the Temporada was moved to Córdoba City.

The winner, Trintignant, about to overtake the Maserati 250F of Gino Munaron.

Results

1949

18 December 1949 – Buenos Aires (RA): Gran Premio del General Juan Perón y de la Ciudad de Buenos Aires – 35 laps/170.275km

N°	Driver	Team	Car	Laps
12	Alberto Ascari (I)	Scuderia Ferrari	Ferrari 166 FL (2.0 sc)	35
16	Juan Manuel Fangio (RA)	ACA	Ferrari 166 FL (2.0 sc)	35
44	Luigi Villoresi (I)	Scuderia Ferrari	Ferrari 166 FL (2.0 sc)	35
6	Benedicto Campos (RA)	ACA	Ferrari 166 FL (2.0 sc)	34
8	José Froilán González (RA)	J Froilán González	Maserati 4CL (1.5 sc)	34
42	B Bira (T)	Scuderia Platè	Maserati 4CLT (1.7 sc)	34
30	Emmanuel de Graffenried (S)	Scuderia Platè	Maserati 4CLT (1.5 sc)	33
10	Dorino Serafini (I)	Scuderia Ferrari	Ferrari 125 C (1.5 sc)	33
28	Clemente Biondetti (I)	L De Filippis	Maserati 4CLT (1.7 sc)	33
40	Peter Whitehead (GB)	P N Whitehead	Ferrari 125C (1.5 sc)	32
46	Louis Chiron (MC)	Helvetic	Maserati 4CLT (1.7 sc)	32
4	Philippe Étancelin (F)	P Étancelin	Talbot T26 C (4.5)	32
26	Eitel Cantoni (ROU)	E Cantoni	Maserati 4CM (1.5 sc)	32
22	Piero Taruffi (I)	Ing P Taruffi	Maserati 4CLT (1.7 sc)	20
2	Nino Farina (I)	Dott G Farina	Maserati 4CLT (1.7 sc)	16
38	Louis Rosier (F)	Écurie Rosier	Talbot T26 C (4.5)	14
36	Piero Carini (I)	P Carini	Maserati 4CLT (1.5 sc)	11
18	Pascual Puopolo (RA)	San Isidoro	Maserati 4CLT (1.5 sc)	9
14	Reg Parnell (GB)	Scuderia Ambrosiana	Maserati 4CLT (1.5 sc)	6
20	Clemar Bucci (RA)	C Bucci	Alfa Romeo 12C-37 (4.6)	5
32	Felice Bonetto (I)	Scuderia Milano	Maserati 4CLT Milano (1.5 sc)	4
24	Oscar Gálvez (RA)	O Gálvez	Alfa Romeo 308 (3.8 sc)	-
34	Manfred von Brauchitsch (D)	San Isidoro	Maserati 8CL (3.0 sc)	-

1950

8 January 1950 – Parco Palermo, Buenos Aires: IV Gran Premio Extraordinario de Eva Duarte Perón – 146.0km (4.87km x 30 laps)

Pos	N°	Driver	Team	Car	Laps
1	44	Luigi Villoresi (I)	Scuderia Ferrari	Ferrari 166 FL (2.0 sc)	30
2	10	Dorino Serafini (I)	Scuderia Ferrari	Ferrari 125 C (1.5 sc)	30
3	20	Clemar Bucci (RA)	C Bucci	Alfa Romeo 12C-37 (4.6)	30
4	16	Juan Manuel Fangio (RA)	ACA	Ferrari 166 FL (2.0 sc)	30
5	32	Felice Bonetto (I)	Scuderia Milano	Maserati 4CLT Milano (1.5 sc)	30
6	2	Nino Farina (I)	Dott G Farina	Maserati 4CLT (1.7 sc)	30
7	38	Louis Rosier (F)	Écurie Rosier	Talbot T26 C (4.5)	30
8	14	Reg Parnell (GB)	Scuderia Ambrosiana	Maserati 4CLT (1.5 sc)	30
9	42	B Bira (T)	Scuderia Platè	Maserati 4CLT (1.5 sc)	30
10	40	Peter Whitehead (GB)	P N Whitehead	Ferrari 125C (1.5 sc)	29
11	28	Clemente Biondetti (I)	L De Filippis	Maserati 4CLT (1.7 sc)	29
12	8	Froilán González (RA)	J Froilán González	Maserati 4CL (1.5 sc)	27
-	46	Louis Chiron (MC)	Helvetic	Maserati 4CLT (1.5 sc)	23
-	26	Eitel Cantoni (ROU)	E Cantoni	Maserati 4CL (1.5 sc)	
-	22	Piero Taruffi (I)	Ing P Taruffi	Maserati 4CLT (1.7 sc)	
-	30	Emmanuel de Graffenried (CH)	Scuderia Platè	Maserati 4CLT (1.7 sc)	
-	4	Philippe Étancelin (F)	P Étancelin	Talbot T26 C (4.5)	16
-	36	Piero Carini (I)	P Carini	Maserati 4CLT (1.5 sc)	
-	12	Alberto Ascari (I)	Scuderia Ferrari	Ferrari 166 FL (2.0 sc)	5
-	6	Benedicto Campos (RA)	ACA	Ferrari 166 FL (2.0 sc)	
-	18	Pascual Puopolo (RA)	San Isidoro	Maserati 4CLT (1.5 sc)	
-	34	Manfred von Brauchitsch (D)	L De Filippis	Maserati 4CLT (1.7 sc)	DNA
-	24	Oscar Gálvez (RA)	O Gálvez	Alfa Romeo 308 (3.8 sc)	DNA

15 January 1950 – El Torreón, Mar del Plata:
III Gran Premio Internacional del General San Martín –
149.7km (4.05km x 37 laps)

Pos	Nª	Driver	Team	Car	Laps
1	12	Alberto Ascari (I)	Scuderia Ferrari	Ferrari 166 FL (2.0 sc)	37
2	2	Nino Farina (I)	Dott G Farina	Maserati 4CLT (1.7 sc)	37
3	22	Piero Taruffi (I)	Ing P Taruffi	Maserati 4CLT (1.7 sc)	37
4	46	Louis Chiron (MC)	Helvetic	Maserati 4CLT (1.5 sc)	36
5	30	Emmanuel de Graffenried (CH)	Scuderia Platè	Maserati 4CLT (1.7 sc)	36
6	8	Froilán González (RA)	ACA	Maserati 4CLT (1.5 sc)	36
7	28	Clemente Biondetti (I)	L De Filippis	Maserati 4CLT (1.7 sc)	36
8	38	Louis Rosier (F)	Ecurie Rosier	Talbot T26 C (4.5)	35
9	42	B Bira (T)	Scuderia Platè	Maserati 4CLT (1.5 sc)	35
10	14	Reg Parnell (GB)	Scuderia Ambrosiana	Maserati 4CLT (1.5 sc)	35
11	4	Philippe Étancelin (F)	P Étancelin	Talbot T26 C (4.5)	35
12	36	Piero Carini (I)	P Carini	Maserati 4CLT (1.5 sc)	33
-	6	Benedicto Campos (RA)	ACA	Ferrari 166 FL (2.0 sc)	13
-	16	Juan Manuel Fangio (RA)	ACA	Ferrari 166 FL (2.0 sc)	12
-	44	Luigi Villoresi (I)	Scuderia Ferrari	Ferrari 166 FL (2.0 sc)	12
-	10	Dorino Serafini (I)	Scuderia Ferrari	Ferrari 125 C (1.5 sc)	3
-	32	Felice Bonetto (I)	Scuderia Milano	Maserati 4CLT (1.5 sc)	2
-	26	Eitel Cantoni (ROU)	E Cantoni	Maserati 4CLT (1.5 sc)	-
-	18	Pascual Puopolo (RA)	San Isidro	Maserati 4CLT (1.5 sc)	-
-	20	Clemar Bucci (RA)	C Bucci	Alfa Romeo 12C-37 (4.6)	-
-	40	Peter Whitehead (GB)	P N Whitehead	Ferrari 125 C (1.5 sc)	-

22 January 1950 – Parque Independencia, Rosario:
IV Copa Acción de San Lorenzo –
140.80km (2.82km x 50 laps)

Pos	N°	Driver	Team	Car	Laps
1	44	Luigi Villoresi (I)	Scuderia Ferrari	Ferrari 166 FL (2.0 sc)	50
2	6	Benedicto Campos (RA)	ACA	Ferrari 166 FL (2.0 sc)	50
3	2	Nino Farina (I)	Dott G Farina	Maserati 4CLT (1.7 sc)	49
4	14	Reg Parnell (GB)	Scuderia Ambrosiana	Maserati 4CLT (1.5 sc)	48
5	20	Clemar Bucci (RA)	C Bucci	Alfa Romeo 12C-37 (4.6)	47
6	4	Philippe Étancelin (F)	P Étancelin	Talbot T26 C (4.5)	47
7	8	Froilán González (RA)	ACA	Maserati 4CLT (1.5 sc)	47
8	26	Eitel Cantoni (ROU)	E Cantoni	Maserati 4CLT (1.5 sc)	47
9	30	Emmanuel de Graffenried (CH)	Scuderia Platè	Maserati 4CLT (1.7 sc)	47
10	18	Pascual Puopolo (RA)	San Isidoro	Maserati 4CLT (1.5 sc)	44
-	16	Juan Manuel Fangio (RA)	ACA	Ferrari 166 FL (2.0 sc)	16
-	10	Dorino Serafini (I)	Scuderia Ferrari	Ferrari 125 C (1.5 sc)	16
-	28	Clemente Biondetti (I)	L De Filippis	Maserati 4CLT (1.7 sc)	13?
-	12	Alberto Ascari (I)	Scuderia Ferrari	Ferrari 166 FL (2.0 sc)	12
-	36	Piero Carini (I)	P Carini	Maserati 4CLT (1.5 sc)	5
-	22	Piero Taruffi (I)	Ing P Taruffi	Maserati 4CLT (1.7 sc)	2
-	32	Felice Bonetto (I)	Scuderia Milan	Maserati 4CLT (1.5 sc)	?
-	48	Ernesto Nanni (RA)	E Nanni	Maserati 4CL (1.5 sc)	DNS

1951

18 February 1951 – Costanera Norte Buenos Aires: V Gran Premio del General Juan Perón y de la Ciudad de Buenos Aires – 157.5km (3.50km x 45 laps)

Pos	N°	Driver	Team	Car	Laps
1	10	Froilán González (RA)	ACA	Ferrari 166 FL (2.0 sc)	45
2	4	Hermann Lang (D)	Daimler-Benz	Mercedes-Benz W154 (3.0 sc)	45
3	2	Juan Manuel Fangio (RA)	Daimler-Benz	Mercedes-Benz W154 (3.0 sc)	45
4	8	Oscar Gálvez (RA)	ACA	Ferrari 166 FL (2.0 sc)	44
5	16	Alfredo Pian (RA)	ACA	Maserati 4CL 1599 (1.5 sc)	44
6	6	Karl Kling (D)	Daimler-Benz	Mercedes-Benz W154 (3.0 sc)	44
7	22	Pascual Puópolo (RA)	-	Maserati	43
8	20	Hector Niemitz (RA)	-	Alfa Romeo (2.9 sc)	42
9	36	Jorge Daponte (RA)	-	Maserati 4CLT (1.5 sc)	42
10	28	Carlos Menditeguy (RA)	J M Fangio	Alfa Romeo 8C 308 (3.8 sc)	41
11	12	José Felix Lopes (RA)	ACA	Simca-Gordini T-15 (1.5)	38
12	24	Clemar Bucci (RA)	-	Alfa Romeo 12C-37 (4.6 sc)	33. DNF
-	14	Luis Alberto de Dios (RA)	ACA	Simca-Gordini T-15 (1.5)	8. DNF
-	32	Roberto Miéres (RA)	-	Maserati (1.5 sc)	2. DNF
-	30	Onofre Marimón (RA)	-	Maserati	DNS
-	26	Alberto Crespo (RA)	-	Maserati	DNS
-	?	Viannini (RA)	-	Maserati 4CL (1.5 sc)	DNA
-	18	Victorio Rosa (RA)	-	Maserati (1.5 sc)	DNA
-	34	Eitel Cantoni (ROU)	-	Maserati 4CL (1.5 sc)	DNA

25 February 1951 – Costanera Norte Buenos Aires: V Gran Premio Extraordinario de Eva Duarte Perón – 157.5km (3.50km x 45 laps)

Pos	N°	Driver	Team	Car	Laps
1	10	Froilán González (RA)	ACA	Ferrari 166 FL (2.0 sc)	45
2	6	Karl Kling (D)	Daimler-Benz	Mercedes-Benz W154 (3.0 sc)	45
3	4	Hermann Lang (D)	Daimler-Benz	Mercedes-Benz W154 (3.0 sc)	43
4	36	Jorge Daponte (RA)	-	Maserati 4CLT (1.5 sc)	43
5	28	Carlos Menditeguy (RA)	J M Fangio	Alfa Romeo 8C 308 (3.8 sc)	35. DNF
-	16	Alfredo Pian (RA)	ACA	Maserati 4CL 1599 (1.5 sc)	23. DNF
-	2	Juan Manuel Fangio (RA)	Daimler-Benz	Mercedes-Benz W154 (3.0 sc)	18. DNF
-	24	Clemar Bucci (RA)	-	Alfa Romeo 12C-37 (4.6 sc)	18. DNF
-	8	Oscar Gálvez (RA)	ACA	Ferrari 166 FL (2.0 sc)	12. DNF
-	14	Luis Alberto de Dios (RA)	ACA	Simca-Gordini T-15 (1.5)	11. DNF
-	20	Hector Niemitz (RA)	-	Alfa Romeo (2.9 sc)	9. DNF
-	22	Pascual Puópolo (RA)	-	Maserati	7. DNF
-	12	José Felix Lopes (RA)	ACA	Simca-Gordini T-15 (1.5)	DNS
-	32	Roberto Miéres (RA)	-	Maserati (1.5 sc)	DNS
-	30	Onofre Marimón (RA)	-	Maserati	DNS
-	26	Alberto Crespo (RA)	-	Maserati	DNS
-	?	Viannini (RA)	-	Maserati 4CL (1.5 sc)	DNA

1953

18 January 1953 – Buenos Aires (RA):
I Gran Premio de la Republica Argentina –
97 laps/379.464km

Pos	N°	Driver	Team	Car	Laps
1	10	Alberto Ascari (I)	Scuderia Ferrari	Ferrari 500	97
2	14	Luigi Villoresi (I)	Scuderia Ferrari	Ferrari 500	96
3	4	José Froilán González (RA)	Officine Alfieri Maserati	Maserati A6GCM-52	96
4	16	Mike Hawthorn (GB)	Scuderia Ferrari	Ferrari 500	96
5	8	Oscar Gálvez (RA)	Officine Alfieri Maserati	Maserati A6GCM-52	96
6	30	Jean Behra (F)	Equipe Gordini	Gordini T16	94
7	28	M Trintignant (F) – H Schell (F)	Equipe Gordini	Gordini T16	91
8	22	John Barber (GB)	Cooper Car Co	Cooper T23 Bristol	90
9	20	Alan Brown (GB)	Cooper Car Co	Cooper T20 Bristol	87
-	26	Robert Manzon (F)	Equipe Gordini	Gordini T16	67. DNF
-	2	Juan Manuel Fangio (RA)	Officine Alfieri Maserati	Maserati A6GCM-52	36. DNF
-	6	Felice Bonetto (I)	Officine Alfieri Maserati	Maserati A6GCM-52	32. DNF
-	12	Nino Farina (I)	Scuderia Ferrari	Ferrari 500	31. DNF
-	32	Carlos Menditeguy (RA)	Equipe Gordini	Gordini T16	24. DNF
-	34	Pablo Birger (RA)	Equipe Gordini	Simca-Gordini T15	21. DNF

1 February 1953 – Buenos Aires (RA):
Gran Premio Ciudad de Buenos Aires –
40 laps/188.277km

Pos	N°	Driver	Team	Car	Laps
1	10	José Farina (I)	Scuderia Ferrari	Ferrari 500 (2.5)	40
2	14	Luigi Villoresi (I)	Scuderia Ferrari	Ferrari 500 (2.5)	40
3	16	Mike Hawthorn (GB)	Scuderia Ferrari	Ferrari 500 (2.5)	40
4	4	José Froilán González (RA)	Officine Alfieri Maserati	Maserati A6GCM-52 (2.0)	40
5	26	Robert Manzon (F)	Equipe Gordini	Gordini T16 (2.0)	39
6	8	Oscar Gálvez (RA)	Officine Alfieri Maserati	Maserati A6GCM-52 (2.0)	39
7	6	Felice Bonetto (I)	Officine Alfieri Maserati	Maserati A6GCM-52 (2.0)	39
8	28	Maurice Trintignant (F)	Equipe Gordini	Gordini T16 (2.0)	38
9	2	Juan Manuel Fangio (RA)	Officine Alfieri Maserati	Maserati A6GCM-52 (2.0)	38
10	56	Onofre Marimón (RA)	ACA	Ferrari 166FL (2.0 sc)	35
11	52	Alberto Crespo (RA)	-	Alfa Romeo 8C-2900A (3.2 sc)	35
12	22	John David Barber (GB)	Cooper Car Co	Cooper T23 Bristol (2.0)	35
13	54	Clemar Bucci (RA)	Clemar Bucci	Alfa Romeo 12C-37 (4.6 sc)	34
14		Roberto Mieres (RA)	Juan M Fangio	Alfa Romeo 8C-308 (3.8 sc)	33
-		José Félix Lopes (RA)	ACA	Ferrari 166FL (2.0 sc)	DNF
-	30	Jean Behra (F)	Equipe Gordini	Gordini T16 (2.0)	DNF
-	32	Carlos Menditeguy (RA)	Equipe Gordini	Gordini T16 (2.0)	DNF
-		Carlos Fortunatti Firpo (RA)	ACA	Maserati 4CLT (1..5 sc)	DNF
-	20	Alan Brown (GB)	Cooper Car Co	Cooper T20 Bristol (2.0)	DNF
-		Remo Gamalero	-	Maserati 4CLT (1.5 sc)	DNF
-	34	Pablo Birger (RA)	Equipe Gordini	Simca-Gordini T15 (1.5)	DNF

1954

17 January 1954 – Buenos Aires (RA):
II Gran Premio de la Republica Argentina –
87 laps/340.344km

Pos	Driver	Team	Car	Time/details
1	Juan Manuel Fangio	Officine Alfieri Maserati	Maserati	3h 00m 55.8s
2	Giuseppe Farina	Scuderia Ferrari	Ferrari	+ 1m 19.0s
3	José Froilán González	Scuderia Ferrari	Ferrari	+ 2m 01.0s
4	Maurice Trintignant	Ecurie Rosier	Ferrari	+ 1 lap
5	Élie Bayol	Equipe Gordini	Gordini	+ 2 laps
6	Harry Schell	Harry Schell	Maserati	+ 3 laps
7	B Bira	Officine Alfieri Maserati	Maserati	+ 4 laps
8	Emmanuel de Graffenried	Emmanuel de Graffenried	Maserati	+ 4 laps
9	Umberto Maglioi	Scuderia Ferrari	Ferrari	+ 5 laps
DSQ	Jean Behra	Officine Alfieri Maserati	Gordini	Outside assistance
DSQ	Mike Hawthorn	Roberto Mieres	Ferrari	Outside assistance
R	Roberto Mieres	Equipe Gordini	Maserati	Engine
R	Onofre Marimón	Jorge Daponte	Maserati	Oil leak
R	Roger Loyer	Ecurie Rosier	Gordini	Oil pressure
R	Jorge Daponte	Scuderia Ferrari	Maserati	Gearbox
R	Louis Rosier	Equipe Gordini	Ferrari	Accident
DNS	Luigi Musso	Onofre Marimón	Maserati	Engine
DNS	Carlos Menditeguy	Officine Alfieri Maserati	Maserati	Engine

Opposite:
24 January 1954 – Buenos Aires (RA):
Round 1. World Sports Car Championship –
106 laps/1004.490km

Abbreviations:

Pos – Finishing position

sc – supercharged

DNA – Did not arrive

DNS – Did not start

DNF – Did not finish

DSQ – Disqualified

NRF – Not running at finish

31 January 1954 – Buenos Aires (RA):
Gran Premio Ciudad de Buenos Aires –
65 laps/305.950km

Pos	Driver	Team	Car	Laps
1	Maurice Trintignant (F)	Ecurie Rosier	Ferrari 625 (2.5)	65
2	Roberto Mieres (RA)	Roberto Mieres	Maserati A6GCM (2.5)	65
3	J F González (RA)/N Farina (I)	Scuderia Ferrari	Ferrari 625 (2.5)	65
4	Harry Schell (USA)	Harry Schell	Maserati A6GCM (2.5)	65
5	Jean Behra (F)	Equipe Gordini	Gordini T16 (2.5)	65
6	Mike Hawthorn (GB)	Scuderia Ferrari	Ferrari 625 (2.5)	64
7	Prince Bira (T)	Officine Alfieri Maserati	Maserati A6GCM (2.5)	64
8	Umberto Maglioli (I)	Scuderia Ferrari	Ferrari 625 (2.5)	64
9	Alfredo Pián (RA)	Alfredo Pián	Ford Pián	57
10	Élie Bayol (F)	Equipe Gordini	Gordini T16 (2.5)	55
-	Onofre Marimón (RA)	Officine Alfieri Maserati	Maserati 250F (2.5)	DNF
-	Juan M Fangio (RA)	Officine Alfieri Maserati	Maserati 250F (2.5)	DNF
-	Nino Farina (I)	Scuderia Ferrari	Ferrari 625 (2.5)	DNF
-	Chico Landi (BR)	Francisco Landi	Ferrari 375 (4.5)	DNF
-	Roger Loyer (F)	Equipe Gordini	Gordini T16 (2.5)	DNF
-	Clemar Bucci (RA)	Clemar Bucci	Alfa Romeo 12C-37 (4.6 sc)	DNF
-	Jorge Daponte (RA)	Jorge Daponte	Maserati A6GCM (2.5)	DNF, A

Pos	Car No	Drivers	Car	Entrant	Laps	DNF Reason	Group	Group Pos
1	10	Giuseppe Farina/Umberto Maglioli	Ferrari 375MM	Scuderia Ferrari	106		Sports +3000	1
2	30	Harry Schell/Alfonso de Portago	Ferrari 250MM Vignale	Alfonso de Portago	103		Sports 3000	1
3	40	Peter Collins/Pat Griffith	Aston Martin DB3S	David Brown	102		Sports 3000	2
4	22	James Scott-Douglas/Ninian Sanderson	Jaguar C-Type	Ecurie Ecosse	100		Sports +3000	2
5	34	Luis Milan/Elpidio Tortone	Ferrari 625TF		99		Sports 3000	3
6	54	Emilio Giletti/Luigi Musso	Maserati A6GCS	Maserati	97		Sports 3000	4
7	12	Louis Rosier/Maurice Trintignant	Ferrari 375	Equipe Louis Rosier	96		Sports +3000	3
8	50	Angel Maiocchi/Lucio Bollaert	Ferrari 225S		87		Sports 3000	5
9	58	Jaroslav Juhan/Antonio Asturias Hall	Porsche 550 Sypder	Jaroslav Juhan	87		Sports 1500	1
10	6	Carroll Shelby/Dale Duncan	Allard-Cadillac J2X	Ray Cherryhomes	86		Sports +3000	4
11	74	Michael Collange/David Speroni	OSCA MT4	OSCA	85		Sports 1500	2
12	64	Oscar J González/Pedro Escudero	Porsche 550		79		Sports 1500	3
13	68	José Sala Herrarte Ariano/Antonio Asturias Hall	Porsche 550 Spyder		79		Sports 1500	4
14	18	Masten Gregory/Dale Duncan	Jaguar C-Type	Masten Gregory	79		Sports +3000	5
15	70	Jorge Chaves/Alberto Rodriguez-Larreta	Porsche 550		72		Sports 1500	5
16	66	Julio Angel Gatti/Juan Antonio Gatti	Porsche 550		70		Sports 1500	6
NRF	32	Roberto Bonomi/Carlos Menditeguy	Ferrari 625TF		91	gearbox	Sports 3000	
DNF	38	Reg Parnell/Roy Salvadori	Aston Martin DB3S	David Brown	65	ignition	Sports 3000	
DNF	60	Hans Hugo Hartmann/Adolf Brudes	Borgward-Hansa 1500RS	Borgward	44	oil system	Sports 1500	
DNF	28	German Pesce/F Molina Zubiria	Jaguar C-Type		38		Sports +3000	
DNF	26	José M Millet/Nicolas Dellepiane	Jaguar C-Type		27		Sports +3000	
DNF	24	Adolfo Schwelm-Cruz/Miguel Schroeder^	Jaguar C-Type	Ecurie Ecosse	26		Sports +3000	
DNF	44	Roberto Mieres/Carlo Tomasi	Aston Martin DB3S	David Brown	24	gearbox	Sports 3000	
DNF	36	Jean Behra/Franco Bordoni	Gordini T24S	Automobiles Gordini	16	engine	Sports 3000	
DNF	30	Ian Stewart/Jimmy Stewart	Jaguar C-Type	Ecurie Ecosse	16	accident	Sports +3000	
DNF	42	Forrest Greene/Carlos Stabile	Aston Martin DB3	E F Greene	14	fatal accident	Sports 3000	
DNF	16	Phil Hill/David M Sykes	Ferrari 340MM	Allen Guiberson	13	clutch	Sports +3000	
DNF	14	José-Maria Ibáñez/Ignacio Janices	Ferrari 375MM		11	accident	Sports +3000	
DNF	4	Franci Bruno/Carlos Bruno	Allard-Cadillac J2X		9		Sports +3000	
DNF	48	Pedro J Llano/Ernesto Tornquist	Ferrari 225E		8	brakes	Sports 3000	
DNF	46	Nicolas Dellepiane/Martin Berasategui	Ferrari 225S		5		Sports 3000	
DNF	72	Bob Said/George Moffett	OSCA MT4	Jack Frierson	5	gearbox	Sports 1500	
DNF	62	Tomas Mayol/J A.Mayol	Porsche 550		2		Sports 1500	
DNF	52	Élie Bayol/Roger Loyer	Gordini T15S	Automobiles Gordini	0	accident	Sports 3000	
DNF	8	Carlos Najurieta/Alberto Gomez	Ford-Maserati V8		0		Sports +3000	
DNS	2	Enrique Sáenz Valiente/Jorge Camano	Cadillac-Arauz	Boliari			Sports +3000	
DNA	56	Luigi Musso/Emanuel de Graffenried	Maserati A6GCS	Maserati			Sports 2000	
DNA		Alejandro de Tomaso/Pedro Suarez	Alfa Romeo				Sports 3000	

Winning Time: 6h41m50.8/149.981kph | **Fastest Lap: Giuseppe Farina (Ferrari 375MM). 3m34.6/158.969kph**

1955

16 January 1955 – Buenos Aires (RA):
III Gran Premio de la Republica Argentina
96 laps – 375.552km

Opposite:
23 January 1955 – Buenos Aires (RA):
Round 1, World Sports Car Championship,
58 laps of a 17.136km circuit – 993.888km

Pos	Drivers	Team	Car	Laps
1	Juan Manuel Fangio (RA)	Daimler Benz AG	Mercedes W196	96
2	González (RA)/Farina (I)/Trintignant (F)	Scuderia Ferrari	Ferrari 625	96
3	Farina (I)/Trintignant (F)/Maglioli (I)	Scuderia Ferrari	Ferrari 625	94
4	Moss (GB)/Kling (D)/Hermann (D)	Daimler Benz AG	Mercedes W196	94
5	Roberto Mieres (RA)	Officine Alfieri Maserati	Maserati 250F	91
6	Harry Schell (USA) Jean Behra (F)	Officine Alfieri Maserati	Maserati 250F	88
7	Musso (I)/Mantovani (I)/Schell (USA)	Officine Alfieri Maserati	Maserati 250F	83
-	Mantovani (I)/Behra (F)/Musso (I)	Officine Alfieri Maserati	Maserati 250F	54, DNF
-	Bucci (RA)/Schell (USA)/Menditeguy (RA)	Officine Alfieri Maserati	Maserati 250F	54, DNF
-	Jesus Iglesias (RA)	Equipe Gordini	Gordini T16	38, DNF
-	Maurice Trintignant (F)	Scuderia Ferrari	Ferrari 625	36, DNF
-	E Castellotti (I)/Luigi Villoresi (I)	Scuderia Lancia	Lancia D50	35, A
-	Stirling Moss (GB)	Daimler Benz AG	Mercedes W196	29, DNF
-	Alberto Uria (U)	A Uria	Maserati A6GCM	22, DNF
-	Alberto Ascari (I)	Scuderia Lancia	Lancia D50	21, A
-	Élie Bayol (F)	Equipe Gordini	Gordini T16	7, DNF

Pos	Car No	Drivers	Car	Entrant	Laps	DNF Reason	Group	Group Pos
1	4	Enrique Sáenz Valiente/José-Maria Ibáñez	Ferrari 375 Plus		58		Sports +3000	1
2	8	Carlos Najurieta/Oscar Rivero	Ferrari 375MM		58		Sports +3000	2
3	30	José M Faraoni/Ricardo Grandio	Maserati A6GCS	Equipo Presidente Peron	56		Sports 3000	1
4	34	Jaroslav Juhan/Jorge Salas Chaves	Porsche 550 Spyder		56		Sports 1500	1
5	14	Élie Bayol/Harry Schell	Gordini T24S	Equipe Gordini	54		Sports 3000	2
6	26	Jorge Camano/Oscar Camano	Ferrari 212		54		Sports 3000	3
7	32	Alejandro de Tomaso/Cesar Reyes	Maserati A6GCS		52		Sports 3000	4
8	52	Oscar Alfredo Gálvez/Eduardo Martins	Ford V8		52		Modified Touring	1
9	18	Luis Milan/Elpidio Tortone	Ferrari 625TF		51		Sports 3000	5
10	50	Juan-Carlos Garavaglia/Manuel Rodriguez	Ford V8		51		Modified Touring	2
11	66	Guillermo G Airaldi/Douglas Marimón	Alfa Romeo 1900		49		Modified Touring	3
12	102	Angel de la Rosa/Angel Antenone	Ford V8		49		Modified Touring	4
13	96	Huge Della Romana	Ford V8		45		Modified Touring	5
14	48	Patricio Badaracco/Ernesto Tornquist	Cisitalia 202		44		Sports 1500	3
15	92	Eugenio Madica/Ignacio Espina	Ford V8		43		Modified Touring	6
16	24	Angel Maiocchi/Carlos Lostalo	Ferrari 225S		42		Sports 3000	6
17	70	Antonio Pereyra/A Cea	Ford V8		42		Modified Touring	7
18	22	Alvaro Piano/Miguel Schroeder/Carlos Alcorta	Ferrari 225E		42		Sports 3000	7
NRF	12	José M Millet/Gabriel Gabin	Jaguar C-Type		41	fuel leak	Sports +3000	
NRF	28	Adolfo Schwelm-Cruz/Pedro J Llano	Gordini T15S	Equipe Gordini	40	gearbox	Sports 3000	
DNF	16	Alberto Rodriguez-Larreta/David Speroni	Ferrari 250MM Pinin Farina			brakes	Sports 3000	
NC	90	Juan VCarrica/J Arias Moreno	Ford V8		39		Modified Touring	8
DNF	20	Umberto Maglioli/Clemar Bucci	Ferrari 750 Monza	Scuderia Ferrari		DSQ	Sports 3000	
DNF	10	Maurice Trintignant/Froilán González	Ferrari 118 LM	Scuderia Ferrari		DSQ	Sports +3000	
DNF	6	Roberto Bonomi/Ernesto Florencio Castro Cranwell	Ferrari 375MM			fuel system	Sports +3000	
DNF	2	Franco Bruno/Carlos Bruno	Allard-Cadillac J2X			brakes	Sports +3000	
NC	38	Curt Delfosse	Gordini-Porsche T15		22		Sports 1500	
DNF	42	Lucio Bollaert/Carlos Stabile	Gordini T15S			gearbox	Sports 1500	
DNF	36	Tomas Mayol/Juan Gabbi	Porsche 356 Super			axles	Sports 1500	
DNF	100	"Carming"/Carlos Guimarey	Ford-Maserati V8				Sports +3000	
DNF	54	Ernesto Petrini/Domingo Colanero	Ford V8				TC	
DNF	56	Felix Alberto Peduzzi/E Del Molino	Chevrolet Bel Air				TC	
DNF	58	Jorge Descote	Ford V8				TC	
DNF	60	Pablo Birger	Ford V8				TC	
DNF	64	Ernesto H Blanco/N Larocca	Ford V8				TC	
DNF	68	Juan Fernando Piersanti/J Colanero	Ford V8				TC	
DNF	74	Juan C Navone/D Teseire	Ford V8				TC	
DNF	76	Marcelo Aloe Vercher/B Marciulevicius	Chevrolet Bel Air				TC	
DNF	78	Elmer J Oppen	Ford V8				TC	

Continues on next page.

23 January 1955 – Buenos Aires (RA): Round 1, World Sports Car Championship *(continued)*

Pos	Car No	Drivers	Car	Entrant	Laps	DNF Reason	Group	Group Pos
DNF	80	Rodolfo de Alzaga/R Luro	Ford V8				TC	
DNF	82	José Lorenzetti	Ford V8				TC	
DNF	84	Enrique D'Ascanio/Hugo Vazquez	Ford V8				TC	
DNF	86	Luis F González/J N Soto	Ford V8				TC	
DNF	88	Plinio Rosetto	Ford V8				TC	
DNF	94	Raul Alonso	Ford V8				TC	
DNF	98	Antonio Gomez	Ford V8				TC	
DNF	104	Francisco de Ridder/Carlo Tomasi	Ford V8				TC	
DNF	106	Segundo Ale/E Canriero	Chevrolet Bel Air				TC	
DNF	110	Emilio Boretto	Ford V8				TC	
DNF	62	Esteban Sokol/E Ojea	Ford V8				TC	
DNF	46	Jorge B Saggese/R Sedano Acosta	Fiat Abarth 207			engine	Sports 1500	
DNF	40	Ernesto Tornquist/Miguel Nadie	Porsche 550 Spyder			accident	Sports 1500	
DNS	44	Oscar J González/Jorge Malbran	Porsche 550 Spyder				Sports 1500	
DNS	72	Tadeo Taddia/Sebastian Messino	Chevrolet Bel Air				TC	
DNS	3	Ernesto Tornquist	Gordini T11S			engine	Sports 1500	
Winning Time: 6h35m15.4/150.872kph				**Fastest Lap: Froilán González (Ferrari 118LM), 6m06.1/168.505kph**				

TC : Turismo Carretera (Modified Touring)

Right:
30 January 1955 – Buenos Aires (RA):
Gran Premio Ciudad de Buenos Aires
60 laps – 282.414km

Pos	Drivers	Team	Car	Laps
1	Nino Farina (I)	Scuderia Ferrari	Ferrari 625 (3.0)	30
2	Juan Manuel Fangio (RA)	Daimler Benz AG	Mercedes W196 (3.0)	30
3	Stirling Moss (GB)	Daimler Benz AG	Mercedes W196 (3.0)	30
4	Karl Kling (D)	Daimler Benz AG	Mercedes W196 (3.0)	30
5	J F González (RA)	Scuderia Ferrari	Ferrari 625 (2.5)	30
6	Roberto Mieres (RA)	Officine Alfieri Maserati	Maserati 250F (2.5)	30
7	Jean Behra (F)	Officine Alfieri Maserati	Maserati 250F (2.7)	30
8	M Trintingnant (F)	Scuderia Ferrari	Ferrari 625 (2.5)	30
9	L Musso (I)/S Mantovani (I)	Officine Alfieri Maserati	Maserati 250F (2.5)	30
10	Carlos Menditeguy (RA)	Officine Alfieri Maserati	Maserati 250F (2.5)	30
11	S Mantovani (I)/H Schell (USA)	Officine Alfieri Maserati	Maserati 250F (2.7)	30
12	Clemar Bucci (RA)	Scuderia Ferrari	Ferrari 625 (2.5)	30
?	Pablo Birger (RA)	Equipe Gordini	Gordini T16 (2.5)	29
?	Élie Bayol (F)	Equipe Gordini	Gordini T16 (2.5)	29
?	Alberto Uria (U)	Alberto Uria	Maserati A6GCM (2.5)	
?	Pián/Faraoni/Schwein Cruz (RA)	-	Maserati A6GCM (2.5)	
?	Jesus Iglesias (RA)	Equipe Gordini	Gordini T16 (2.5)	
-	Hans Hermann (D)	Daimler Benz AG	Mercedes W196 (2.5)	18
-	Umberto Maglioli (I)	Scuderia Ferrari	Ferrari 118LM (3.7)	-

1956

22 January 1956 – Buenos Aires (RA):
IV Gran Premio de la Republica Argentina –
98 laps – 383.376km

Pos	Drivers	Team	Car	Laps
1	Juan Manuel Fangio (RA)/Luigi Musso (I)	Scuderia Ferrari	Lancia D50 Ferrari	98
2	Jean Behra (F)	Officine Alfieri Maserati	Maserati 250F	98
3	Mike Hawthorn (GB)	Owen Racing Organisation	Maserati 250F	96
4	Chico Landi (BR)/Gerino Gerini (I)	Officine Alfieri Maserati	Maserati 250F	92
5	Olivier Gendebien (B)	Scuderia Ferrari	Ferrari 555	91
6	Oscar González (RU)/Alberto Uria (RU)	Alberto Uria	Maserati A6GCM	88
-	Stirling Moss (GB)	Officine Alfieri Maserati	Maserati 250F	81, DNF
-	Peter Collins (GB)	Scuderia Ferrari	Ferrari 555	58, DNF
-	Luigi Piotti (I)	Officine Alfieri Maserati	Maserati 250F	57, DNF
-	Carlos Menditeguy (RA)	Officine Alfieri Maserati	Maserati 250F	42, DNF
-	Eugenio Castellotti (I)	Scuderia Ferrari	Lancia D50 Ferrari	40, DNF
-	José Froilán González (RA)	Officine Alfieri Maserati	Maserati 250F	24, DNF
-	Juan Manuel Fangio (RA)	Scuderia Ferrari	Lancia D50 Ferrari	22, DNF

5 February 1956 – Mendoza:
Gran Premio Ciudad de Buenos Aires –
60 laps – 251.05km

Pos	Driver	Team	Car	Laps
1	Juan Manuel Fangio (RA)	Scuderia Ferrari	Lancia D50 Ferrari	60
2	Stirling Moss (GB)	Officine Alfieri Maserati	Maserati 250F	60
3	Jean Behra (F)	Officine Alfieri Maserati	Maserati 250F	60
4	Carlos Menditéguy (RA)	Officine Alfieri Maserati	Maserati 250F	59
5	Peter Collins (GB)	Scuderia Ferrari	Ferrari 555	58
6	Olivier Gendebien (B)	Scuderia Ferrari	Ferrari 555	57
7	Chico Landi (BR)	Officine Alfieri Maserati	Maserati 250F	57
8	Pablo Gulle (RA)	Officine Alfieri Maserati	Maserati 250F	54
9	Mike Hawthorn (GB)	Owen Racing Organisation	Maserati 250F	54
10	Luigi Piotti (I)	Officine Alfieri Maserati	Maserati 250F	52
-	Eugenio Castellotti (I)	Scuderia Ferrari	Lancia D50 Ferrari	14, DNF
-	Luigi Musso (I)	Scuderia Ferrari	Lancia D50 Ferrari	9, DNF
-	Alberto Uria (U)	Alberto Uria	Maserati A6GCM	DNS

29 January 1956 – Buenos Aires (RA):
Round 1, World Sports Car Championship –
106 laps of a 9.476km circuit – 1004.490km

Pos	Car No	Drivers	Car	Entrant	Laps	DNF Reason	Group	Group Pos
1	31	Stirling Moss/Carlos Menditeguy	Maserati 300S	Officine Alfieri Maserati	106		Sports 3000	1
2	36	Olivier Gendebien/Phil Hill	Ferrari 857 Monza	Scuderia Ferrari	104		Sports +3000	1
3	32	Froilán González/Jean Behra	Maserati 300S	Officine Alfieri Maserati	101		Sports 3000	2
4	4	Alejandro de Tomaso/Carlo Tomasi	Maserati 150S		97		Sports 1500	1
5	20	Enrique Muro/Julio Pola	Ferrari 500 Mondial		93		Sports 2000	1
6	26	Eduardo Kovacs-Jones/Raul Jaras	Mercedes-Benz 300SL		90		Sports 3000	3
7	6	Isabel Haskell/Carlos Lostalo	Maserati 150S		88		Sports 1500	2
8	24	Angel Maiocchi/Lucio Bollaert	Ferrari 225S		85		Sports 3000	4
9	49	Franco Bruno/Carlos Bruno	Allard-Cadillac J2		71		Sports +3000	2
NRF	43	Juan Manuel Fangio/Eugenio Castellotti	Ferrari 410 Sport	Scuderia Ferrari	89	gearbox	Sports +3000	
NRF	1	Jaroslav Juhan/José F Lopes	Porsche 550 Spyder		72	accident	Sports 1500	
DNF	3	Curt Delfosse/Pedro Escudero	Gordini-Porsche T15		70	DSQ	Sports 1500	
DNF	33	Francisco Landi/Gerino Gerini	Maserato 300S		68	engine	Sports 3000	
DNF	44	Luigi Musso/Peter Collins	Ferrari 410 Sport	Scuderia Ferrari	61	gearbox	Sports +3000	
DNF	42	Roberto Bonomi/Ernesto Florencio Castro Cranwell	Ferrari 375MM		59	fire	Sports +3000	
DNF	34	Luis Milan/Ela Capotosti	Ferrari 625TF		44	clutch	Sports 3000	
DNF	41	Celso Lara-Barberis/Godofredo Vianna	Ferrari 375		41	engine	Sports +3000	
DNF	30	Lino Fayen/Joao Rozende Dos Santos	Ferrari 750 Monza		37	axle	Sports 3000	
DNF	45	Enrique Sáenz Valiente/Jorge Camano	Ferrari 375 Plus		35	overheating	Sports +3000	
DNF	22	Maria-Teresa de Filippis	Maserati A6GCS		26	accident	Sports 2000	
DNF	46	Carlos Najurieta/Cesar Rivero	Ferrari 375MM		23	gearbox	Sports +3000	
DNF	5	Miguel Jantus/Alberto Gomez	Gordini T15S		22	engine	Sports 1500	
DNF	23	Ricardo Grandio/Alberto Rodriguez-Larreta	Maserati A6GCS		21		Sports 2000	
DNF	25	Danilo Ciapessoni/Cesar Reyes	Ferrari 225E		16	engine	Sports 3000	
DNF	2	Tomas Mayol/Juan Gobbi	Porsche 550 Spyder		14	engine	Sports 1500	
DNF	21	Osvaldo Carballido/Elias Carballido	Austin-Healey 100M		11	fire	Sports 3000	
DNF	35	José M Millet/Miguel Schroeder	Jaguar C-Type		3		Sports +3000	
DNS	40	Jean Blanc/Colette Duval/Pedro J Llano	Talbot-Lago T26 GS				Sports +3000	
DNA	7	Arturo Santamarina/David Speroni	Alfa Romeo 1900				Sports 2000	
DNA	37	Carlos Guimarey/Caralpey	Alfa Romeo				Sports 3000	
DNA	47	Gaston Perkins/Rodolfo de Alzaga	Maserati-Ford A6G				Sports +3000	
DNA	48	Clemar Busci/Pedro Suarez	Alfa Romeo 12C 37				Sports +3000	
Winning Time: 6h29m37.9/154.683kph			**Fastest Lap: Peter Collins (Ferrari 410 Plus), 3m26.4/165.285kph**					

1957

13 January 1957 – Buenos Aires (RA):
V Gran Premio de la Republica Argentina –
100 laps – 391.2km

Pos	Drivers	Team	Car	Laps
1	Juan Manuel Fangio (RA)	Officine Alfieri Maserati	Maserati 250F	100
2	Jean Behra (F)	Officine Alfieri Maserati	Maserati 250F	100
3	Carlos Menditeguy (RA)	Officine Alfieri Maserati	Maserati 250F	99
4	Harry Schell (USA)	Scuderia Centro Sud	Maserati 250F	98
5	J F González (RA)/A de Portago (E)	Scuderia Ferrari	Lancia D50 Ferrari	98
6	Perdisa (I)/Collins (GB)/von Trips (D)	Scuderia Ferrari	Lancia D50 Ferrari	98
7	Jo Bonnier (S)	Scuderia Centro Sud	Maserati 250F	95
8	Stirling Moss (GB)	Officine Alfieri Maserati	Maserati 250F	93
9	Alessandro de Tomaso (RA)	Scuderia Centro Sud	Ferrari 500	91
10	Luigi Piotti (I)	L Piotti	Maserati 250F	90
-	Eugenio Castellotti (I)	Scuderia Ferrari	Lancia D50 Ferrari	75, DNF
-	Mike Hawthorn (GB)	Scuderia Ferrari	Lancia D50 Ferrari	35, DNF
-	Luigi Musso (I)	Scuderia Ferrari	Lancia D50 Ferrari	31, DNF
-	Peter Collins (GB)	Scuderia Ferrari	Lancia D50 Ferrari	26, DNF

27 January 1957 – Buenos Aires (RA):
XI Gran Premio Ciudad de Buenos Aires –
60 laps – 273.96km

Pos	Drivers	Car	Team	VtS
1	Juan Manuel Fangio (RA)	Maserati 250F	Officine Alfieri Maserati	60
2	Jean Behra (F)	Maserati 250F	Officine Alfieri Maserati	60
3	Luigi Musso (I)/Peter Collins (GB)	Lancia D50 Ferrari	Scuderia Ferrari	60
4	Mike Hawthorn (GB)	Lancia D50 Ferrari	Scuderia Ferrari	60
5	Egenio Castelotti (I)/Luigi Musso (I)	Lancia D50 Ferrari	Scuderia Ferrari	60
6	Carlos Menditéguy (RA)/Stirling Moss (GB)	Maserati 250F	Officine Alfieri Maserati	60
7	Cesare Perdisa (I)	Lancia D50 Ferrari	Scuderia Ferrari	59
8	Wolfang von Trips (D)/Peter Collins (GB)	Lancia D50 Ferrari	Scuderia Ferrari	59
9	Alejandro de Tomaso (RA)/Luigi Piotti (I)	Maserati 250F	L Piotti	55
10	Harry Schell (USA)	Maserati 250F	Scuderia Centro Sud	51
-	Peter Collins (GB)/Mastern Gregory (USA)	Lancia D50 Ferrari	Scuderia Ferrari	40
-	Enrique Sticconi (RA)	Maserati 250F	Scuderia Centro Sud	29
-	Stirling Moss (GB)	Maserati 250F	Officine Alfieri Maserati	24
-	José Froilán González (RA)	Ferrari 625	José Froilán González	23
-	Giorgio Scarlatti (I)	Maserati 250F	Scuderia Centro Sud	3

20 January 1957 – Buenos Aires (RA):
Round 1, World Sports Car Championship –
98 laps of 10.219km circuit – 1001.462km

Pos	Car No	Drivers	Car	Entrant	Laps	DNF Reason	Group	Group Pos
1	10	Masten Gregory/Eugenio Castellotti/Luigi Musso/Giuseppe	Ferrari 290MM	Scuderia Temple Buell	98		Sports +3000	1
2	28	Jean Behra/Carlos Menditeguy/Stirling Moss	Maserati 300S	Officine Alfieri Maserati	98		Sports 3000	1
3	8	Alfonso de Portago/Peter Collins/Eugenio Castellotti/Wolfgang von Trips	Ferrari 290MM	Scuderia Ferrari	98		Sports +3000	2
4	14	Roberto Mieres/Ninian Sanderson	Jaguar D-Type	Ecurie Ecosse	95		Sports +3000	3
5	16	Roberto Bonomi/Luigi Piotti/Miguel Schroeder	Maserati 350S	Officine Alfieri Maserati	91		Sports +3000	4
6	62	Alejandro de Tomaso/Isabel Haskell	OSCA MT4	OSCA	88		Sports 1500	1
7	52	Piero Drogo/Julio Pola	Ferrari 500 Testa Rossa	Madunina Venezuela	87		Sports 2000	1
8	68	Jaroslav Juhan/Antonio von Doery	Porsche 550 RS Carrera	Jaroslav Juhan	86		Sports 1500	2
9	36	Herminio Ferreira Filho/Godofredo Vianna	Ferrari 750 Monza	Sao Paulo Automovil Club	85		Sports 3000	2
10	50	Carlos Danvila/Omar Terra	Mercedes-Benz 300SL	Orlando Terra	78		Sports 3000	3
11	48	Nestor Salerno/Cesar Reyes	Ferrari 212 Inter	Nestor Salerno	74		Sports 3000	4
12	70	Curt Delfosse/Ernesto Tornquist	Porsche 550 RS Carrera	Curt Delfosse	71		Sports 1500	3
NRF	56	Severino Silva/Pinheiro Piris	Maserati 300S	Scuderia Madunina Brasil	90	accident	Sports 2000	
NRF	38	Celso Lara-Barberis/Eugenio Martins	Ferrari 750 Monza	Scuderia Madunina Brasil	91	engine	Sports 3000	
DNF	64	Sergio Vivaldi/Lino Fayen	OSCA MT4	Venezuela Sports Group	65	engine	Sports 1500	
DNF	2	Stirling Moss/Juan Manuel Fangio	Maserati 450S	Officine Alfieri Maserati	57	gearbox	Sports +3000	
DNF	4	Eugenio Castellotti/Wolfgang von Trips/Luigi Musso/Mike Hawthorn	Ferrari 290S	Scuderia Ferrari	55	ignition	Sports +3000	
DNF	18	Luis Milan/Jorge Camano	Ferrari 375 Plus	Argentina Racing	51	gearbox	Sports +3000	
DNF	66	Christian Bino Heins/Cyro Cayres	Porsche 550 RS	Scuderia Madunina Brasil	45	gearbox	Sports 1500	
DNF	30	Harry Schell/Jo Bonnier	Maserati 300S	Officine Alfieri Maserati	25	clutch	Sports 3000	
DNF	58	Enrique Arrieta/Carlos Guimarey	OSCA MT4		14	engine	Sports 2000	
DNF	6	Peter Collins/Mike Hawthorn/Eugenio Castellotti	Ferrari 290S	Scuderia Ferrari	2	oil pressure	Sports +3000	
DNF	54	Oscar Camano/Miguel Jantus	Maserati A6G		1	accident	Sports 2000	
DNF	34	Oscar Cabalen/Carlo Tomasi	Maserati 300S	Scuderia Madunina Brasil	1	accident	Sports 3000	
DNS	32	Giorgio Scarlatti/Juan Manuel Fangio	Maserati 250S	Officine Alfieri Maserati		withdrew	Sports 3000	
DNS	20	Carlos Najurieta/Cesar Rivera	Ferrari 375MM	Argentina Racing		accident	Sports +3000	
DNS	12	Ron Flockhart/Roberto Mieres	Jaguar D-Type	Ecurie Ecosse		accident	Sports +3000	
DNS	22	Clemar Bucci/Oscar de Petris	Ferrari 375MM	Argentina Racing		accident	Sports +3000	
DNS	40	Alvaro Piano/Franco Bruno	Ferrari 625TF				Sports 3000	
DNS	26	Carlos Bruno/Angel Pinotti	Allard-Cadillac J2	Argentina Racing			Sports +3000	
Winning Time: 6h10m29.9/161.181kph				Fastest Lap: Stirling Moss (Maserati 300S), 3m47.6/170.317kph				

1958

Overleaf:
26 January 1958 – Buenos Aires (RA):

19 January 1958 – Buenos Aires (RA):
VI Gran Premio de la Republica Argentina –
80 laps – 312.96km

Pos	Driver	Team	Car	Laps
1	Stirling Moss (GB)	R R C Walker Racing Team	Cooper T43 Climax	80
2	Luigi Musso (I)	Scuderia Ferrari	Ferrari 246	80
3	Mike Hawthorn (GB)	Scuderia Ferrari	Ferrari 246	80
4	Juan Manuel Fangio (RA)	Scuderia Sud Americana	Maserati 250F	80
5	Jean Behra (F)	Ken Kavanagh	Maserati 250F	78
6	Harry Schell (USA)	Jo Bonnier	Maserati 250F	77
7	Carlos Menditeguy (RA)	Scuderia Sud Americana	Maserati 250F	76
8	Paco Godia Sales (E)	Francisco Godia Sales	Maserati 250F	75
9	Horace Gould (GB)	H H Gould	Maserati 250F	71
-	Peter Collins (GB)	Scuderia Ferrari	Ferrari 246	0

2 February 1958 – Buenos Aires (RA):
XIV Gran Premio Ciudad de Buenos Aires –
60 laps – 282.414km

Pos	Driver	Car	Team	Laps
1	Juan Manuel Fangio (RA)	Maserati 250F	Scuderia Sud Americana	60
2	Luigi Musso (I)	Ferrari 246	Scuderia Ferrari	60
3	Carlos Menditeguy (RA)	Maserati 250F	Francisco Godia Sales	59
4	Scarlatti (I) – Jean Behra (F)	Maserati 250F	Ken Kavanagh	57
5	Jo Bonnier (S)	Maserati 250F	Jo Bonnier	57
6	José Froilán González (RA)	Ferrari Chevrolet	J F González	57
7	Ramón Requejo (RA)	Chevrolet Special	R Requejo	56
8	Marcos Galván (URGY)	Ford Special	M Galván	55
9	Danton Bazet (URGY)	Chevrolet Special	D Bazet	54
10	Asdrúbal Fontes-Bayardo (URGY)	Maserati-Chevrolet	A Fontes-Bayardo	51
11	Horace Gould (GB)	Maserati 250F	H H Gould	40
-	Peter Collins (GB)	Ferrari 246	Scuderia Ferrari	-
-	Mike Hawtorn (GB)	Ferrari 246	Scuderia Ferrari	-
-	Wolfgang von Trips (D)	Ferrari 246	Scuderia Ferrari	-
-	Roberto Bonomi (RA)	Maserati 250F	R Bonomi	-
-	Ken Kavanagh (AUS)	Maserati 250F	Ken Kavanagh	-
-	Stirling Moss (GB)	Cooper T43 Climax	R R C Walker Racing Team	-
-	Jesús Iglesias (RA)	Chevrolet Special	J Iglesias	-
-	Roberto Miéres (RA)	Maserati 250F	Scuderia Sud Americana	-

26 January 1958 – Buenos Aires (RA):
Round 1, World Sports Car Championship –
106 laps of a 9.476km circuit – 1004.490km

Pos	Car No	Drivers	Car	Entrant	Laps	DNF Reason	Group	Group Pos
1	2	Peter Collins/Phil Hill	Ferrari 250 TR58	Scuderia Ferrari	106		Sports 3000	1
2	4	Wolfgang von Trips/Olivier Gendebien	Ferrari 250 TR58	Scuderia Ferrari	106		Sports 3000	2
3	48	Stirling Moss/Jean Behra	Porsche 550 RS 1.6		106		Sports 2000	1
4	26	Piero Drogo/Sergio González	Ferrari 250 TR	Piero Drogo	102		Sports 3000	3
5	50	Edgar Barth/Roberto Miéres/Anton von Döry	Porsche 550 RS		99		Sports 1500	1
6	34	Gino Munaron/Luciano Mantovani	Ferrari 500 TR		98		Sports 2000	2
7	28	Luis Milan/Antonio Mendes de Barros	Maserati 300S [3035]		98		Sports 3000	4
8	10	Maurice Trintignant/François Picard	Ferrari 250 GT LWB		97		Sports 3000	5
9	44	Ricardo Grandio/Eduardo Kovacs-Jones	Osca F2/S 1500		95		Sports 1500	2
10	52	Jaroslav Juhan/Hubert Wiesse	Porsche 550 RS		94		Sports 1500	3
11	38	Julio Guimarey/Carlos Guimarey	Maserati A6G		80		Sports 2000	3
NRF	42	Roberto Bonomi/Luigi Piotti	Osca FS1500		75	Gearbox	Sports 1500	
DNF	40	Alberto Rodriguez-Larreta/Maria-Teresa de Filippis	Osca TN1500		71	Electrics	Sports 1500	
DNF	24	Celso Lara-Barberis/Eugenio Martins	Ferrari 750 Monza		57	Engine	Sports 3000	
DNF	32	Jo Bonnier/Masten Gregory	Maserati 200SI		47	Brakes	Sports 2000	
DNF	22	Alvaro Piano/Franco Bruno	Ferrari 625TF		42	Accident	Sports 3000	
DNF	36	Gerino Gerini/Giuseppe Musso	Maserati 200SI		30	Fuel system	Sports 2000	
DNF	62	Stuart Monro/Eduardo Dibos-Chappuis	Mercedes-Benz 300SL		30	Differential	Sports 3000	
DNF	12	Juan Manuel Fangio/Francisco Godia-Sales	Maserati 300S	Scuderia Centro Sud	24	Accident damage	Sports 3000	
DNF	54	Pedro von Döry/Curt Delfosse	Porsche 550		21	Gearbox	Sports 1500	
DNF	20	Patricio Badaracco/Federico Mayol	Aston Martin DB2		15	Accident	Sports 3000	
DNF	30	Giorgio Scarlatti/Antonio Negri Bevilacqua	Maserati 200SI		15	Accident	Sports 2000	
DNF	14	Jorge Magnasco/Juan-Manuel Bordeu	Maserati 300S		8	Fatal accident	Sports 3000	
DNF	8	Johnny von Neumann/Wolfgang Seidel	Ferrari 250 TR		7	Rear axle	Sports 3000	
DNF	46	Alejandro de Tomaso/Isabelle Haskell/Carlo Tomasi	Osca F2/S 1500		5	Axle	Sports 1500	
DNF	6	Luigi Musso/Mike Hawthorn	Ferrari 250 TR	Scuderia Ferrari	0	Accident	Sports 3000	
DNS		Alberto Gomez	Lancia D23				Sports 3000	
DNS	16	Stirling Moss/Jean Behra	Maserati 300S	Scuderia Centro Sud		Engine	Sports 3000	
DNS	56	Tomas Mayol/Osvaldo José Mantega	Porsche 550				Sports 1500	
DNS	58	Horacio Durado/Horacio Carlomagno	Simca Huit				Sports 1500	
Winning Time: 6h19m55.4/158.636kph				**Fastest Lap: Peter Collins (Ferrari 250 Testa Rossa), 3m25.9/165.686kph**				

1960

21 January 1960 – Buenos Aires (RA):
Round 1, World Sports Car Championship –
106 laps of a 9.476km circuit – 1004.490km

Pos	Car No	Drivers	Car	Entrant	Laps	DNF Reason	Group	Group Pos
1	4	Phil Hill/Cliff Allison	Ferrari 250 Testa Rossa 59/60	Scuderia Ferrari	106		Sports 3000	1
2	2	Richie Ginther/Wolfgang von Trips	Ferrari 250 Testa Rossa 59/60	Scuderia Ferrari	105		Sports 3000	2
3	30	Jo Bonnier/Graham Hill	Porsche 718 RSK	Porsche KG	101		Sports 1600	1
4	14	Celso Lara-Barberis/Christian Bino Heins	Maserati 300S		101		Sports 3000	3
5	42	Pedro von Döry/Anton von Döry/Juan-Manuel Bordeu	Porsche 718 RSK		100		Sports 1600	2
6	36	Christian Goethals/Curt Delfosse	Porsche 718 RSK		100		Sports 1600	3
7	34	Maurice Trintignant/Hans Herrmann	Porsche 718 RSK	Porsche KG	95		Sports 1600	4
8	44	Hugo Maestretti/Alberto Gomez	Porsche 718 RSK		94		Sports 1600	5
9	50	Bruno Gavazzoli/Nino Todaro	Ferrari 250 GT Interim		92		Grand Touring	1
10	56	Huschke von Hanstein/Heriberto Bohnen	Porsche 356B Carrera	Porsche KG	88		Grand Touring	2
11	52	Ugo Tosa/Silvano Turco	Ferrari 250 GT		83		Grand Touring	3
NRF	8	Roberto Bonomi/Luis Milan	Maserati 300S		83	Clutch	Sports 3000	
DNF	20	Dan Gurney/Masten Gregory	Maserati Tipo 61 Birdcage	Camoradi International	56	Gearbox	Sports 3000	
DNF	32	Olivier Gendebien/Edgar Barth	Porsche 718 RSK	Porsche KG	53	Oil pipe	Sports 1600	
DNF	6	Ludovico Scarfiotti/Froilán González	Ferrari Dino 246S	Scuderia Ferrari	38	Distributor	Sports 3000	
DNF	10	Rodolfo de Alzaga/Nestor Salerno	Maserati 300S		10	Engine	Sports 3000	
DNF	24	Antonio Pucci/Ernesto Dagnino	Maserati		5	Oil pressure	Sports 3000	
DNF	18	Camilo Gay/Cesar Rivero	Lancia D24		4	Transmission	Sports 3000	
DNF	54	Carlo Maria Abate/Alberto Rodriguez-Larreta/Carlos Menditéguy	Ferrari 250 GT		2	Brakes	Grand Touring	
DNF	16	Fernando Barreto/Carlos Najurieta	Maserati 300S			Transmission	Sports 3000	
DNF	22	Enrique Sticoni/Jésus-Ricardo Iglesias	Maserati 200SI			Gearbox	Sports 3000	
DNF	40	Harry Blanchard/Wolfgang Seidel	Porsche 718 RSK	Wolfgang Seidel		Fatal accident	Sports 1600	
DNF	38	Heini Walter/Juan-Manuel Bordeu	Porsche 718 RSK			Accident	Sports 1600	
DNS	26	Ettore Muro Chimeri/Julio Pola	Maserati 300S				Sports 3000	
DNS	12	Carlos Guimarey/Antonio Creus	Maserati 300S				Sports 3000	
DNS	28	Cesar Reyes/Julio Guimarey	Ferrari 750 Monza				Sports 3000	
DNS	48	Carlo Maria Abate/Casimiro Toselli	Ferrari 250 GT				Grand Touring	
DNS	46	Gino Munaron/Carlos Reyes/Alberto Mapelli Mozzi	OSCA 1500S				Sports 1600	

Winning Time: 6h17m12.1/159.780kph — **Fastest Lap: Dan Gurney (Maserati Tipo 61), 3m22.4/168.551kph**

7 February 1960 – Buenos Aires (RA):
VII Gran Premio de la Republica Argentina –
80 laps – 3.912km

Pos	Driver	Entrant	Laps
1	Bruce McLaren	Cooper-Climax T51	80
2	Cliff Allison	Ferrari D246	80
3=	Maurice Trintignant	Cooper-Climax T51	
3=	Stirling Moss	Cooper-Climax T51	80
4	Carlos Menditeguy	Cooper-Maserati T51	80
5	Wolfgang von Trips	Ferrari D246	79
6	Innes Ireland	Lotus-Climax 18	79
7	Jo Bonnier	BRM P25	79
8	Phil Hill	Ferrari D246	77
9	Rodriguez Larreta	Lotus-Climax 16	77
10	Froilán González	Ferrari D246	77
11	Roberto Bonomi	Cooper-Maserati T51	76
12	Masten Gregory	Behra Porsche-Porsche	76
13	Gino Munaron	Maserati 250F	72
14	Nasif Estefano	Maserati 250F	70
	Harry Schell	Cooper-Climax T51	63
	Jack Brabham	Cooper-Climax T51	42
	Stirling Moss	Cooper-Climax T51	40
	Graham Hill	BRM P25	37
	Alan Stacey	Lotus-Climax 16	24
	Ettore Chimeri	Maserati 250F	23

14 February 1960 – Córdoba:
XIII Buenos Aires Grand Prix –
75 laps – 255.000km

Pos	Driver	Entrant	Laps
1	Maurice Trintignant	Cooper-Climax T51	75
2	Dan Gurney	BRM P25	75
3	Gino Munaron	Maserati 250F	70
4	Innes Ireland	Lotus-Climax 18	70
5	Ettore Chimeri	Maserati 250F	68
6	Carlos Menditeguy	Cooper-Maserati T51	63
7	Jo Bonnier	BRM P25	53
	Harry Schell	Cooper-Climax T51	
	Froilán González	Ferrari D246	
	Bruce McLaren	Cooper-Climax T51	
	Innes Ireland	Lotus-Climax 18	
	Alan Stacey/António Creus	Maserati 250F	
	Roberto Bonomi/Masten Gregory	Behra-Porsche	

More titles from Veloce:

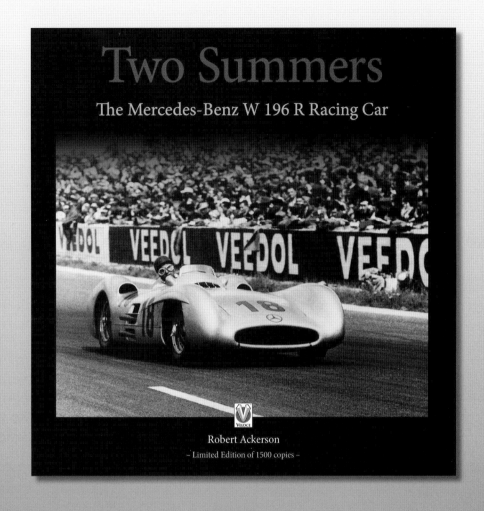

The story of the Mercedes-Benz W 196 R Grand Prix racing car – its development, roots, and magnificent two-year racing career – has enough drama, emotion and excitement to fill a dozen books, but only this volume captures the car's enduring greatness. Hundreds of photos from the Daimler archives, stunning original artwork, and written with authority, reflection and admiration for the W 196 R.

ISBN: 978-1-845847-51-7
Hardback • 25x25cm • £75* UK/$125* USA • 192 pages • 171 colour and b&w pictures

For more info on Veloce titles, visit our website at www.veloce.co.uk • email: info@veloce.co.uk • Tel: +44(0)1305 260068
* prices subject to change, p&p extra

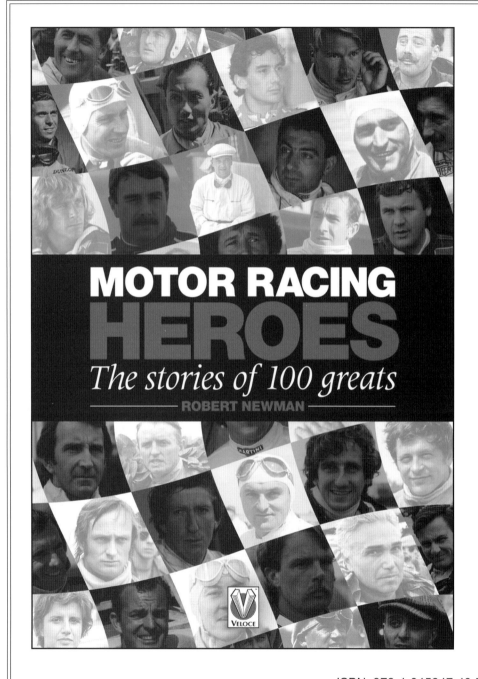

MOTOR RACING HEROES
The stories of 100 greats
ROBERT NEWMAN

Stories about 100 heroes from almost 100 years of motorsport fill this book. Revealing the determination, heroism, raw courage, skill at the wheel – and just plain humanity – that has elevated men and women into the special, rarified atmosphere of heroism.

Stories of memorably brave deeds, as well as a few light-hearted tales, include those of Alberto Ascari, André Boillot, Robert Benoist, William Grover Williams, Jean-Pierre Wimille, Maria Teresa de Felippis, David Purley, Alessandro Zanardi, Giannino Marzotto and Giovanni Bracco, in this fascinating collection.

ISBN: 978-1-845847-48-7
Hardback • 21x14.8cm • £19.99* UK/$32.99* USA • 384 pages • pictures

* prices subject to change, p&p extra

BUGATTI
Type 57 Grand Prix
– A Celebration

A. Williams

Neil Max Tomlinson

VELOCE

A comprehensive, radical look at the history and development of the Type 57 Grand Prix Bugattis. New material challenges traditional beliefs about these historic cars, and rejects some long-standing conventions. Myths are explored and truths are revealed in this work celebrating all aspects of these remarkable cars and their creators.

ISBN: 978-1-845847-89-0
Hardback • 24.8x24.8cm • £50* UK/$85* USA • 176 pages • 158 colour and b&w pictures

For more info on Veloce titles, visit our website at www.veloce.co.uk • email: info@veloce.co.uk • Tel: +44(0)1305 260068
* prices subject to change, p&p extra

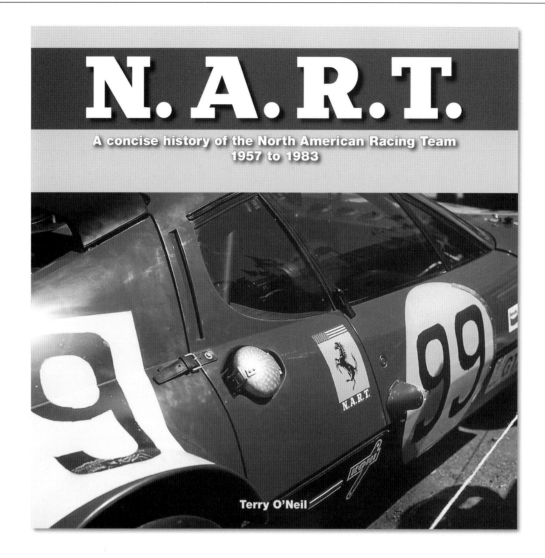

Luigi Chinetti's association with Ferrari, and the origins, formation and racing history of NART.
A complex organisation, inextricably linked to Luigi Chinetti Motors Inc, NART enjoyed success on
the race tracks of the US and Europe for three decades – despite financial difficulties and arguments
with organisers – to rightly become a legend.

ISBN: 978-1-845847-87-6
Hardback • 24.8x24.8cm • £60* UK/$100* USA • 256 pages •
295 colour and b&w pictures

For more info on Veloce titles, visit our website at www.veloce.co.uk
• email: info@veloce.co.uk • Tel: +44(0)1305 260068
* prices subject to change, p&p extra

Index